27.7.96.
To Dad,

a phenomenal Humorist !

Well Done.
love from Freia
xx

THE MUNRO PHENOMENON

PHENOMENON

Andrew Dempster

MAINSTREAM
PUBLISHING

EDINBURGH AND LONDON

In memory of Bill Houlsby

First published in Great Britain in 1995 by
MAINSTREAM PUBLISHING COMPANY (EDINBURGH) LTD
7 Albany Street
Edinburgh EH1 3UG

ISBN 1 85158 698 9

A catalogue record for this book is available from the British Library

Typeset in Ehrhardt by Litho Link Ltd, Powys, Wales

Printed in Spain by AGT, Toledo

D.L.TO:94-1995

Contents

Looking along Glen
Lochay to Creag
Mhor

*Great things are done when men and mountains meet; This is not done by
jostling in the street.*

William Blake

Freedom of the hills

*Mine is the freedom of the tranquil hills
When vagrant breezes bend the sinewy grass,
While sunshine on the widespread landscape spills
And light as down the fleet cloud-shadows pass.*

*Mine, still, that freedom when the storm clouds race,
Cracking their whips against defiant crags
And mists swirl boiling up from inky space
To vanish on the instant, torn to rags.*

*When winter grips the mountains in a vice,
Silently stifling with its pall of snow,
Checking the streams; clasping the rocks in ice,
Still to the mantled summits I would go.*

*Sun-drenched, I sense the message they impact,
Storm-lashed, I hear it sing through every vein;
Among the snows it whispers to my heart
'Here is your freedom. Taste – and come again!'*

Douglas Fraser

ACKNOWLEDGMENTS

A book of this nature would have been impossible to write without the physical and literary input of dozens of people who have effectively created 'the Munro phenomenon'. In particular, I would like to thank Hamish Brown for his valuable contributions, information and advice throughout the latter stages.

My thanks are due to Derek Pyper, the slide custodian of the Scottish Mountaineering Club, for allowing me to use slides from the SMC collection. I am also indebted to Mrs Maud Tiso and the SMC secretary John Fowler for the use of several slides from A.E. Robertson's extensive collection.

The following have all supplied (directly or indirectly) either photographs, permission to use quotes, information or advice, and a heartfelt thankyou goes out to each and every one:

Adrian Belton, Alastair Borthwick, W.D. Brooker, Hamish Brown, Jon Broxap, Craig Caldwell, Robin Campbell, Jim Crumley, Mike Cudahy, Alan Dawson, Douglas Fraser, Rory Gibson, Muriel Gray, Dave Hewitt, Robert Howard, Andrew Johnstone, Martin Moran, Kathy Murgatroyd, W.H. Murray, Mark Rigby, Douglas Scott, Martin Stone, Hugh Symonds, Paul Tattersall, Tom Weir and Heather Wilson.

Finally, I wish to thank Alexandrina Robertson for her patient typing of the manuscript.

FOREWORD

by

Hamish Brown

Most of the books in the small library of Munroitis are either concerned with some of the more notable feats in 'bagging' Munros or are simply guide-books, ranging from the simple pocket size to coffee-table glossies. Most Munroists will possess most if not all of this collection – and here is another!

The Munro Phenomenon is different. While including an account of one 'ordinary' man's round (with which *all* will associate), it is largely a history of the activity and an attempt to analyse the compulsions and philosophies that lie behind the phenomenon. As such, it effectively fills a gap and, to the Munroist, will be compulsive reading. 'All you ever wanted to know about Munros and Munroing' could be its subtitle.

When I made the first continuous round it was very much a fun trip. Certainly there were the necessities of pertinacity and fitness, etc., but the walk was kept on schedule so when the 112 days was touted (by newspapers of course) as a 'record' I was not pleased. Martin Moran's winter timetable was not aiming for a 'record' either, but it was, of course, and a new Munro phenomenon was born: the sporting, competitive, record-breaking aspect. It is one I find astonishing, and justifiable, a reminder of the agony of aspiring that is part of man's nature. When someone does the Munros in a month I will shake my head – and his hand. There are no moral high grounds in Munro games. It is all daft and we must live and let live.

At the time of *Hamish's Mountain Walk* (in the title I avoided the very word Munro, but lost the fight against my name being there) Munroing was at a low ebb – OS maps had gone metric, everything was being re-surveyed, old orders were dying, the historic 'Tables' might even be dropped. Yet more people had more leisure time. The book fell into those rather still waters and set off some ripples, which now bear more likeness to a tidal wave. Heavens! The word Munro can be used across the floor of the House of Commons without needing to be explained. Munros are for everyone.

A book giving objective coverage is an achievement in a world which delights in introverted acrimony and debate. I, you, we, may not agree with everything in the following pages but it is a fair attempt at showing the past and explaining the present.

Few will realise the long and painstaking research that Andrew Dempster has had to put in (using precious Munros' time): checking the facts, contacting people involved, tracing elusive photographs, writing and rewriting. The result is a work which will be around for a long time as the definitive story of Munroing. A dinner celebrating the centenary of the publication of the 'Tables' crowded a hotel venue. I wonder what stadium will be required for the next obvious celebration in the year 2001.

If that date has no significance then you are a very new Munroist or a very ignorant one. Not for long: this book tells all, mercifully free of pretensions or tabloid sensationalism. After all, it is mostly just about a healthy and happy recreational activity which just happened to bumble into becoming a phenomenal phenomenon. I feel it an honour to be asked to write a foreword. Foreworded is forewarned, however. Every copy of the 'Tables' should carry a health warning: Munros are good for us.

INTRODUCTION

It has been estimated that around 40,000 people in Scotland are regular hillwalkers. The figure for the whole of Britain is obviously much higher, and a conservative 'guesstimate' indicates that at least 100,000 people are actively engaged in climbing Munros – i.e., Scottish mountains over 3,000 feet. Further, this figure is continually increasing and it is now known that well over 1,000 individuals have completed all 277 Munros. The sport of 'Munro-bagging' has now reached such dizzy heights of popularity that articles have appeared in *The Times* magazine about it, and even a television series has been made extolling its healthy virtues. The former Labour Leader the late John Smith was a confessed Munro addict with over a hundred to his name when he died, and he even kept a map of Munros he had climbed on the wall of his office off Parliament Square. The word *Munro* is now entering the common English vocabulary, and in fact is explained in *The Oxford Guide to English Usage*.

This volume is not another guide-book to climbing the Munros but instead explores the foundations and features of the present-day Munro phenomenon. Who exactly was Hugh Munro? Why has Munro-bagging become so popular? Why climb Munros at all? This book will attempt to answer all these questions and more by delving deeply into the ethos behind this almost cult pursuit, in addition to a detailed examination of its origins and history. From the early exploits of Sir Hugh Munro himself to the super-charged present-day fell-running feats of Hugh Symonds, the following chapters will cover the whole spectrum of this widespread pursuit with particular emphasis on the human side. In short, it sets the Munro phenomenon in its wider context.

This book should be of obvious interest to anyone who is currently working their way through Munro's list and indeed to those seasoned veterans who have accomplished their quest and are perhaps searching for a more solid background to their personal achievement. It should also be of interest to 'armchair' Munro-baggers who have no intention of slogging their way up a 3,000-foot peak but nevertheless have a genuine interest in the growing outdoor phenomenon and the associated Munro-mania.

In addition to investigating the ethos and history of Munro-bagging, this volume also attempts to address the many important issues which are central to its very nature and existence. The twin and sometimes conflicting aims of wilderness conservation and rights of public access, together with wider implications, are discussed fully in Chapter 10. The confused technical distinctions between Munros and Tops and the relatively recent controversial revisions of Munro's Tables in the early Eighties are discussed in Appendix 1. The great 'safety debate' is of prime importance as more and more people flock to the hills – and subsequently more accidents happen. Appendix 2 deals thoroughly with this aspect and recent mountain rescue issues.

The heart of this book is in effect not Munros but the people who climb them, and perhaps the title should be changed to 'The Munro-Bagger Phenomenon'. As such, it is far removed from the practical where-to-park, how-to-climb guide-book and essentially fills the gap between this and the human aspect. Contrary to popular opinion, not all Munro-baggers are bearded males with glasses. Men and women, young and old, husbands and wives, fathers and sons, even dogs, all climb Munros and gain immense satisfaction and enjoyment from doing so. They have been done in single expeditions in summer and winter, stretched out to last a lifetime or ran round in less than two months. Doctors and decorators, teachers and preachers, lawyers and labourers and even television presenters and politicians have all become obsessed with 'doing the Munros'. As well as John Smith, another Labour MP, Chris Smith, has actually completed the round and become the first MP to do so. As multi-Munroist Hamish Brown points out, it is a British trait to treat politics as a joke and sport seriously, whether the sport may be football or Munro-bagging. For many Munro addicts their sport can assume the utmost importance in their lives, eventually leading to a cult obsession. Staunch Tory Sir Hugh Munro would probably have been quite disconcerted to learn that the first MP to complete his Munros should belong to the Labour Party, but then as Chris Smith remarks and 100,000 others echo, there is at least one Tory to whom we shall all be forever grateful.

CHAPTER 1

Sir Hugh Munro

The Lost Leader

Just for a handful of summits he left us,
Just for a 'Dearg' to tick on his list.
Thus Munro's Tables have slowly bereft us,
Changed Ultramontane to Salvationist.
Raeburn was with us, Collie was of us,
Ling, Glover were for us – they watch from belays.
He alone breaks from the van and the freemen,
Climbs up his mountains the easiest ways.

We shall climb prospering – not thro' his presence,
Leads will inspirit us – not on his rope.
Deeds will be done while he boasts his collection,
Ben Vane to Braeriach, Mount Keen to Ben Hope.
Blot out his name then, record one lost soul more,
One more peak-bagger to collar them all.
Pelt him with pitons and crown him with crampons,
Leave him spreadeagled on Rubicon Wall!

Douglas Fraser

In December 1890 a lone Victorian figure dressed in knickerbockers, Inverness cape and Balmoral bonnet, carrying a long ice-axe and aneroid, dragged his heavy hobnail boots through deep powder snow and thick mist to reach the bland summit of Carn na Caim, a 3,000-foot mountain lying south-east of Dalwhinnie. On arrival at the cairn, he took out the aneroid to check the height and made a few scribbles in his notebook. The time was just 10 a.m., but by 1.15 p.m. he had caught the train to Glasgow, ending a three-day skirmish in the rolling hills around Dalwhinnie.

That evening the lightly built, bearded 33-year-old had swapped his baggy knickerbockers for a smart kilt to attend the annual dinner of the

Sir Hugh T. Munro,
the man who
started it all

Scottish Mountaineering Club, formed only the year before. The man was
Hugh Munro, and he had previously written in the *SMC Journal*:

> I should be glad at almost any time during January, February and March
> to join small parties of members of the club on expeditions of one or
> several days' duration. I am willing to go anywhere, but the districts I
> am most anxious to explore are – the Sutherland hills, the Ullapool and
> Loch Maree country, the Cuchuillins, Western Inverness-shire, the
> Blackmount, Glencoe, Glen Nevis and Glen Lyon hills. During the
> months mentioned I can almost always find time for a trip, but later I
> am much engaged. I am sometimes free, however, for a few days, and if
> it fitted my movements I would be glad to join any climbing party on
> learning of it.
>
> H.T. Munro, Lindertis

It will be apparent from the above extract that many of Hugh Munro's long mountain jaunts took place during winter owing to his other commitments. This certainly did not lessen Munro's enthusiasm however, in fact quite the contrary, and his series of articles entitled 'Winter Ascents' in the early editions of the *SMC Journal* are irrefutable proof of his finer appreciation of the Scottish peaks when under snow and ice. To quote:

> It cannot be denied that some few disadvantages attend winter and early spring climbing, but I am sure that all who have tried it will agree that the pleasure derived is more than ample compensation.
> (H.T. Munro, *SMC Journal*, volume 1, 1890)

Yet many would fail to see the pleasure that Munro derived from the day of 22 January 1891 when he battled through snow and wind from Blair Atholl to Kirkmichael via the three Munros of Beinn a' Ghlo, a distance of over 20 miles, which even in summer would have been considered a long expedition. On the summit ridge the snow was blowing 'in spiral columns several hundred feet high, penetrating everything, filling pockets and drifting between waistcoat and shirt, where it melted and then froze into a solid wedge of ice. In all my winter experience I never suffered so severely from cold.'

Yet despite the severe weather he still managed to perform the technicalities of aneroid measurements and topographical descriptions. He continues:

> Heavy walking all day in soft snow. At Diranean they had to scrape me down with a knife to get the frozen snow off me before I could enter the house.

These were the days of heavy wool and tweeds. Multi-layer fleecy clothing 'systems', light Goretex shells and other 'breakthroughs' in boot and rucksack technology were still a life-time away.

But what was this man really like? What were his qualities, interests and aspirations? The man who brought about his *Tables of Heights Over 3,000 Feet* in 1891 scarcely realised then that his very name would soon become synonymous with all Scottish mountains over 3,000 feet and that he would become a legendary figure in Scottish mountaineering.

Hugh Thomas Munro was born in London in 1856, the eldest of nine children and the son of Sir Campbell Munro of Lindertis. His family were Scots and during his childhood he spent some of his time in London and the rest in the house of 'Drumleys' three miles south of Kirriemuir on the southern edge of the Eastern Grampians. The old family home was in the estate of Lindertis, lying three miles west of Kirriemuir, which Munro eventually inherited in 1913. Lindertis is a 3,000-acre estate and 260-acre farm which is still going strong today, being famous for its pedigree bulls. The old mansion house of Lindertis, the start of many of Munro's mountain wanderings, is sadly now all but a ruin, the main building being unroofed due to the expense of constant repairs.

As a child, Munro's great delight was in collecting things such as fossils, shells, eggs and butterflies. This 'collecting' tendency continued into adulthood, when as a young man he returned after a trip to South Africa with an interesting collection of Basuto curios, antelope heads, a black boy and a monkey! Indeed his predisposition to collecting partly explains his consequent desire to 'collect' 3,000-foot summits.

Munro's South African trip was just one of many to countless parts of the world and in his early life travel played an enormous part, both for business and pleasure. In fact, his first introduction to the mountains was in Germany in his late teens when he was a student in Stuttgart. His business training and ordered mind stood him in good stead in later years for classifying the Scottish peaks and managing the estate at Lindertis.

Munro was a warm and sociable person and a notable musician, enjoying Wagner and also showing much skill on the flute. He could dance well and was a great talker. Munro was enthusiastic about anything he undertook and also something of a perfectionist, as is certainly evident in the detailed notes he produced on the Scottish hills. His love of change and variety were perfectly suited to his job of a King's Messenger, a professional courier who carried foreign despatches for diplomats. In 1880, when he was still only 24, he joined Sir George Colley, Governor of Natal, as his private secretary and eventually served with a cavalry corps in the Basuto War.

When back in Britain, he spent most of his time at Lindertis, managing the estate. This was his true home, and the Highland hills on his doorstep became his 'spiritual home' no matter how far he travelled. When Munro was 29 he stood as parliamentary Tory candidate for Kirkcaldy Burghs in Fife but he never stood for his local Forfar seat. He married but his wife died ten years later and most of his life was spent as a widower. His children often went with him in his various ventures to America, Japan, Morocco and Europe.

Munro was an original member of the Scottish Mountaineering Club at its conception in 1889 and at this time he had already gleaned much experience of climbing the Scottish hills. It was generally believed then that only some 30 Scottish peaks were over 3,000 feet in height – the 'definitive' *Baddely's Guide* listed only 31! The first *SMC Journal*, however, indicated that there may be ten times this number, 'some perhaps never ascended'.

These words acted as a stimulus to Munro: he was the obvious person to catalogue and climb them, and this he did with much enthusiasm and passion. The resulting *Tables of Height Over 3,000 Feet*, published in 1891, became the most famous document in Scottish mountaineering history and has since had eight separate revisions and republications.

Munro was duly elected as president of the SMC from 1894 to 1897 and there are over 80 entries in the club journal written by him, many describing topographical details which were not present on any maps of the period. Indeed, it was another 80 years before the Ordnance Survey managed to produce accurate and reliable maps of parts of the north-west Highlands! One such part is the great wilderness area lying between Loch Maree and Little Loch Broom now known as the Fisherfield Forest. Scattered within its confines are some of the most inaccessible and remote peaks in Scotland, one of these, A'Mhaighdean (the Maiden), is commonly regarded as the remotest Munro. Munro himself did not make the ascent of A'Mhaighdean until Easter Sunday 1900, which according to Munro 'was certainly not a tempting day for the hills – the worst of a very wet week'. This at least confirms that Easter weather was still as bad then as it is now! In his article 'A'Mhaighdean' Munro comments: 'Its very name is probably only known to a few of our members, whilst fewer still have ever climbed it. Even the Ordnance surveyors do not seem to have mapped the district with their usual care, for while the six-inch map gives no height to the Maiden, the one-inch map only gives a 2,750-foot contour.' His suspicion that the mountain exceeded 3,000 feet had been partly validated by two other SMC members who had both estimated its height at about 3,100 feet. He continues: 'For many years I have desired to make this ascent, because of its remoteness, because of its commanding position in the centre of a most beautiful and interesting district, and, last but not least, to determine as far as may be its true height.' An interesting footnote on the same page indicates that on the OS map of the time for 'the whole of the southern portion of the Teallach range, which is only about six miles to the NNE of the Maiden, not a single height is given'.

It is abundantly clear from these observations that the OS maps of the time, while reliable for many areas, were notoriously patchy in more remote districts. Hugh Munro's topographical notes and aneroid readings made a vital contribution to subsequent cartography of these wilderness areas of Scotland.

Munro goes on to describe his expedition to climb A'Mhaighdean with his two companions, H.G.S. Lawson and W.N. Ling, the latter a fairly influential member of the SMC. They began at Kinlochewe 'in a pretty persistent downpour' and proceeded to the head of Lochan Fada via the Heights of Kinlochewe and Gleann na Muice. Munro describes the view from Lochan Fada thus:

The view from here is very striking and alone is well worth the two-and-a-quarter hours which it took to reach it, the cluster of hills round the head of Lochan Fada grouping as well as anything I have seen in Scotland – notably the black, frowning northern precipice of Beinn Lair. We did not, however, see the view until our return, for the hills were shrouded in mist and the rain had turned by this time into sleet.

Luckily, by the time they had trudged along the trackless north shore of Lochan Fada and hit the south shoulder of the mountain the mist had cleared off and the sun was out. On reaching the summit in heavy and drifting snow, they revelled in the fine views and descended to the loch in 35 minutes, where they discovered unanimously from three aneroid readings that the mountain was 2,060 feet above the loch. Knowing that the loch was at 1,000 feet, they concluded that the height of A'Mhaighdean was 3,060 feet.

Munro's Tables today list the height as 967m, or 3,172 feet, though the contours on the OS 1:50,000 map indicate a height of just over 3,083 feet – quite a difference! In fact this confusion over heights produced two new Munros in this area as late as 1974. One, Ruadh Stac Mor, lies less than a mile north-west of A'Mhaighdean and scrapes the magic line by a mere 11 feet. The other, Beinn A' Chlaidheimh, lays claim to being the smallest Munro, at a height of exactly 3,000 feet. Finally, Beinn Tarsuinn was checked by aneroid measurements in 1929 by Corbett and Inglis and found to be 3,077 feet. Yet it was still a *footnote* in the Tables in 1953. Today it assumes its rightful place as a Munro at 3,071 feet.

Munro's real passion was for long cross-country routes through remote areas, often lasting several days. Although he enjoyed company, many of these trips were undertaken alone and there can be no doubt that he also enjoyed his own company. In those days, of course, there were no lightweight one-man tents and the mountain bothies used by today's hillwalking fraternity were either occupied by families, in a ruinous state or kept permanently locked by estate owners to be used in the stalking season. Munro relied on the goodwill of Highland people to put him up at night and by all accounts this was particularly forthcoming.

Typical of these Highland jaunts was the week in February 1889 when he took the boat to Inverie in the remote Knoydart peninsula, where the local laird put him up in the lodge. Incidentally, the little hamlet of Inverie is as remote now as it was then and no roads connect it with the 'outside world'. Its little pub, the Forge, is considered to be the remotest in Britain, as is its post office and shop.

The following day Munro crossed the high pass known as Mam Barrisdale to the fiord-like Loch Hourn, which he thought of as the most

SMC meet at Dalwhinnie. Munro is on the extreme left

beautiful of Scottish lochs. There he stayed in a rather grimy hut which could offer little more than oatmeal and foul whisky! He continued on up to Glen Quoich Lodge, which is now under water – drowned by Loch Quoich in one of the post-war hydro-electrification schemes which have tragically permanently disfigured many Scottish glens. At the lodge he had lunch with the factor before being given a lift to Fort Augustus.

The next day he took the Loch Ness steamer to Drumnadrochit and continued west on foot to Glen Cannich with an overnight stop at Guisachan. From Glen Cannich (another sad casualty of hydro-electrification) he traversed the massive bulk of Mam Sodhail and Sgurr na Lapaich to eventually arrive at Shiel Inn on Loch Duich via the Falls of Glomach – an incredibly long day for February. Based at the inn, he had a day on the Five Sisters of Kintail. Finally, he went over the steep Mam Ratagan pass, climbed Beinn Sgritheall and ended at Glenelg, where the steamer *Clansman* took him to Glasgow and the sleeper train to London.

In these pre-car, pre-hydro days it is amazing how Munro managed to accomplish as much as he did. His passionate enthusiasm for wild country knew no bounds and was the overriding factor in his continued success and survival. He firmly believed that there was nothing dangerous about

17

climbing mountains alone and the 'never-go-alone' rules of today's cosseted urbanites certainly didn't apply to him. Nevertheless, on a February crossing of the Cairngorms when mist suddenly came down and froze on his clothes, hair and beard he realised it was 4.30 p.m. and he was only in the vicinity of remote Ben Macdui. Light was fading and 'the cold so intense that one could scarcely have lived an hour without moving'. In addition, his normally accurate compass work had somehow brought him down 1,000 feet of icy hillside to the edge of dangerous cliffs. He had no option but to retrace his steps back up the mountain and take another bearing. This time he found himself even worse off. Many lesser mortals by this time would have panicked and no doubt become another hillwalking statistic. Munro, however, calmed his nerves and pulled out his map to work out his position. Now it was third time lucky and at 6 p.m. he found himself on the shores of frozen Loch Etchachan over 3,000 feet above sea level and in almost pitch dark. By 8.30 p.m. he had trudged down Glen Derry and was hospitably entertained at Lui Beg by the head stalker and his wife.

It will be apparent by this time that Hugh Munro had an inner strength and determination coupled with a good deal of 'mountain-sense', essential for a man who exposed himself to the elements on so many occasions. In the final analysis it is experience that wins the day and Munro certainly had no shortage of that.

However, Munro's impeccable reputation was to suffer a setback in March 1900 a few days after his A'Mhaighdean trip when he was staying at the Aultguish Inn at the eastern end of Loch Glascarnoch. A rather late after-lunch start had been made up Strath Vaich to the lonely Munro of Am Faochagach. On the route down he spent much time step-cutting and then found that he could not cross a swollen stream. He detoured to a keeper's house, where he borrowed a horse and subsequently arrived back at the inn after midnight.

More severe problems occurred the following day when, in the company of H. Lawson, he 'bagged' four of the Fannichs before descending northwards to Loch a' Bhraoin. Again, they had difficulty fording a stream and the failing light caused them to lose their bearings and suffer consequent benightment. The three matches in their possession offered little help and they spent the night unsuccessfully attempting to locate the road in freezing conditions. (Moral: always carry a torch in winter.) Finally, at 7 a.m. they reached the road, where Munro's driver was still patiently waiting with a fire lit and hot cocoa on the go!

One of Munro's great ambitions was to visit the isle of Rum, which he duly did on 4 February 1891. This was the start of another eventful Highland foray. At this time Rum was a closed book to mountaineers and even today it has rather a mysterious air about it, access being granted only by permission from the Nature Conservancy Council. In the Munro spirit of things he traversed the Rum Cuillin ridge in a day, which even in summer is considered to be a full day.

Munro left Rum in an open boat for Arisaig, where he set off to traverse the peaks of Glen Finnan and Lochaber. After some unusual spring-like conditions on Rum, he left the stage-house in Glenfinnan in dreadful weather. (The stage-house is now the Stagehouse Hotel.) He remarks: 'Fifteen miles down to Corpach Hotel in wild wind and sheets of rain. Members will be taken at this homely and comfortable inn at 8s 6d a day.'

The following day he ascended Carn Mor Dearg in better conditions but did not continue along the narrow arête to Ben Nevis. Instead, he descended to the col below the Aonachs, having to cut steps with his ice-axe (no crampons then). As it was getting late, he headed back to Corpach.

His final mountain day that trip was a visit to the Mamores on the other side of Glen Nevis, where he made a successful traverse of the narrow An Gearannach ridge. On the descent he met a forester who greeted him with the words 'But that was a terrible place you were on.' Apparently, the forester had seen Munro from below and had come up to take home his mangled corpse! The following day Munro headed for home aboard *The Fusilier*, marking the end of yet another successful venture.

Munro was an avid user of the West Highland railway, which was having its heyday before the motor car began to make its presence felt in the early 1900s. Munro at once saw its potential and commented: 'Without doubt the motor car offers possibilities, and brings within the scope of a day or two's expedition regions which formerly, even with the help of a bicycle, would have taken thrice as long.'

One such region, which formed the basis of an article in volume 12 of the *SMC Journal*, was the mountainous area between Loch Nevis and Loch Quoich, which Munro described as 'certainly among the most inaccessible in the kingdom'. He makes the point that without a car the best plan would be to take a boat to Inverie in Knoydart and then to the head of Loch Nevis, depositing the climber at the foot of Sgurr na Ciche. Incidentally, this is the location of Sourlies Bothy, not surprisingly one of the most popular bothies in Scotland, giving access to some of the remotest and most rugged peaks in the Highlands. Note that at this time there was no drivable road along the north side of Loch Arkaig. From Sgurr na Ciche an almost unbroken ridge runs eastwards on the south side of the present Loch Quoich for over nine miles with five Munros on its serpentine switchback crest. The only appreciable drop is before the last Munro, Gairich. Even today this is one of the wildest, most unfrequented ridge-walks in Scotland, situated in an uninhabited tract of desolate terrain.

Munro explains that from the summit of Gairich it is an easy walk of one and a half hours to the footbridge over the Garry just below Loch Quoich. From here it is six miles to Tomdoun, which provided the title for his article. Since the abandonment of the Spean Bridge-Fort Augustus railway (even in his day) reliance on a train would only have allowed him to reach Tomdoun very late at night by a 26-mile drive after the arrival of the 9.06 p.m. train at Spean Bridge. Yet with the car 'J, Rennie and I left home at 12.30 and were at Tomdoun in comfortable time for dinner.'

Those of us today who complain about the A9 road from Perth to Inverness would do well to listen to Munro's remarks about the roads then. 'The road from Blair Atholl to Dalwhinnie we found surprisingly good. The rough stones which covered it about a year ago had, to a large extent, been removed.' The road along Loch Laggan he described as 'scandalously bad' and between Spean Bridge and Invergarry as moderate, except at two places with noticeboards indicating three and seven 'water-courses across roadway' respectively. He continues: 'Above Invergarry the road is stony, narrow and twisty, and requires careful driving. Beyond Tomdoun it is considerably worse, and between Bunchaolie and Kinlochquoich it is very bad.'

Sourlies Bothy

20

In the summer of 1912 Munro had four good hill days from his base at Tomdoun, the longest involving the ridge mentioned above though only as far as Sgurr Mor (four Munros). It is ironic that due to the enlargement of Loch Quoich with hydro-electrification, access to these Munros today is harder now than it was then – certainly by the Loch Quoich approach. Even from the road-end at Loch Arkaig an extremely long summer day would be needed to accomplish the same four Munros. Of course, the double irony is that despite this inaccessibility, these mountains probably see more visitors in a single summer season today than in the whole of Hugh Munro's lifetime. One wonders if Munro had any conception of the deluge to follow. Later on in the same article, Munro says: 'The hotel is plain, simple and comfortable, and the food good, patronised mainly by fishing people, who return year after year. The ordinary tourist element is (thank goodness) not met with.' Tomdoun today is still very much a fisherman's hotel but sees its fair share of the 'tourist element' and Munro-baggers, though many of the latter elect to camp out and sample the real 'wilderness experience'.

Munro was 56 on this Tomdoun trip and only seven years of his life were left. During his very active life the Scottish hills had played a large part, and the Scottish Mountaineering Club was the natural outlet for the narration of his experiences both in print and verbally during long after-dinner speeches. The SMC obviously meant a lot to Munro and on his election to president in 1894 he said that he held the honour in higher esteem than if he had been made Prime Minister of Great Britain. He only failed to attend a club meet on a handful of occasions and in his younger days came from far-flung corners of the earth just to attend a meet.

In the early days of the club two fairly distinctive, but not mutually exclusive, types of mountaineer began to emerge, so called 'Salvationists' and 'Ultramontanes', between which much friendly rivalry ensued. The first group were basically hillwalkers who climbed mountains by their easiest routes and only engaged in any rockwork if it was absolutely necessary. As Hely Almond described them in volume 2 of the club journal, 'We like to know that we are safe – absolutely safe. We don't like contusions; we would rather go home to dinner than lie on the ground till people came to set our bones, or carry us off on a stretcher; we have no desire to be the conscious element of an avalanche or land-slip.' There is a touch of irony here in that by far the majority of mountaineering accidents today involve hillwalkers; with rock-climbers and other serious climbers in the minority. This second group, the 'Ultramontanes', were 'those whose ambition is to scale the inaccessible side of peaks with unpronounceable names, who look upon a quarry face with fond enthusiasm'.

Members of the 'Salvation Army', the Salvationists, included such redoubtables as Hugh Munro, Joseph Stott and Archibald Robertson, and today most Munro-baggers would fall into this category. Although it would be wrong to assume that Hugh Munro never attempted any rock-climbs, his preference lay in the Salvationist tendency. Traditionally it has been commonly regarded that Munro failed to climb two of the mountains on his list, the Inaccessible Pinnacle on Skye and Carn Cloich-Mhuilinn in the Cairngorms, which he was keeping for his last as it was close to his home and therefore more suited to a final Munro celebration. A common misconception about Munro was that, being a Salvationist, he did not possess the required technical competence to climb the Inaccessible Pinnacle. By all accounts nothing could be further from the truth. In 1906 he climbed the Pinnacle Ridge of Sgurr nan Gillean, which is a good deal longer and harder than the Inaccessible Pinnacle. The real bogey was in fact the Skye weather, which was just as much a problem then as it is now. In 1895 he had to leave Skye in abysmal conditions and in 1897 during the memorable Yachting Meet the boat could not even anchor in Loch Scavaig due to the wild weather. Arrangements with Harold Raeburn (the Ultramontane of his day) in 1905 fell through and he was even there as late as 1915 but with no success.

At this point it should be mentioned that in addition to the 277 Munro mountains in Scotland there exists a second class of 240 lesser 3,000-foot summits called Tops. (For a detailed discussion of Munros and Tops see Appendix 1.)

It is reasonable to ask whether Munro was attempting to climb all the Tops or was only interested in the Munros. All the facts point to the former and it is notable that he never missed the opportunity of visiting a Top when the situation arose. The official historical record stated that Munro had climbed all the Tops except the Inaccessible Pinnacle and Carn Cloich-Mhuilinn. An interesting point to note here is that the Pinnacle was listed as an ordinary Top in the original list and Carn Cloich-Mhuilinn as a full Munro. Today the situation is the exact reverse! It is understandable that the 'In. Pin.' should have full Munro status as it is higher than the parent summit of Sgurr Dearg, but it is strange that Hugh Munro himself let it pass as a Top in the first edition of the Tables. It is also rather galling to think that the summit which Munro was saving for his last 'Munro' has now been demoted to a Top!

To complicate the issue still further, there is ample evidence to indicate that Munro actually had three Tops still to climb. In 1917 he remarked, 'I still aspire to stand on the summit of the only three "Tops" in Scotland exceeding 3,000 feet in height which I have not yet climbed. Raeburn, Collie, Garden and others, however, must combine to haul me up on a rope; otherwise the ascents will not be made!'

This last comment does not refer to any lack of technical ability on the part of Munro but rather to his rheumatism, which was a recurrent affliction throughout most of his life. Indeed, as early as 1893, when Munro was only 37, there is a report of him having to turn back on a crossing from Glen Clova to Glen Muick because of this very condition.

So which other Top had Munro still to climb? A check made on Munro's personal copy of the Tables indicated Carn an Fhidhleir at the head of Glen Feshie (another contender for remotest Munro) to be unclimbed. In fact, the second person to complete the Munros, Ronald Burn, visited Munro at Lindertis in January 1919, only two months before Munro's death, and determined at that time that Munro had still to climb three Tops – the two previously mentioned and Carn an Fhidhleir.

This failure on Carn an Fhidhleir, as with the Inaccessible Pinnacle, certainly wasn't due to lack of trying. An attempt on 11 July 1908 in torrential rain and *darkness* was described by Munro's companion, William Garden. They had approached from the south by way of Glen Tilt and at 11 p.m. reached the remains of an old shepherd's bothy, where they 'rigged up a tent with a mackintosh, under which we took our bearings by aid of compass, map, and matches'. On the ascent they hit thick mist but by 1.05 a.m. had reached the large summit cairn of An Sgarsoch, another Munro lying roughly two miles east of Carn an Fhidhleir. 'It was now quite chilly, very dark, and, what was worse, we had been unable to keep our powder dry, and so could neither read our compass nor see our maps.'

As a result, they abandoned the idea of continuing to Carn an Fhidhleir, which in Garden's words 'was more regretted by Munro than I, because in consequence it still remains one of the few three-thousanders undone by him'.

But why had they chosen to make the ascent under cover of darkness? It turns out that Munro made many other ascents at night, the reason probably being that he had a strict, almost fanatical, recognition of the exclusive rights of landowners and didn't like to be seen wandering on what he recognised as private land. Being a landowner himself (and a Tory), Munro adopted an unyielding position regarding rights of exclusion and by all accounts was the prime mover in forming the rather compliant policies of the Scottish Mountaineering Club concerning land access.

Although Munro never accomplished his dream of finishing the Tops, he at least had the privilege of hosting an SMC meet at his home at Lindertis, an ambition of his for many years. Two memorable meets were held there in 1915. This was during the First World War, of course, and although Munro was past military age he went out to Malta in 1914 to work for the Red Cross. In 1918, after the war, he and two daughters organised a canteen for troops in Tarascon in Provence and in the following spring he developed a chill. This subsequently took Munro's life when pneumonia took over and he died on 19 March 1919 aged 63. A report in the local French paper goes as follows:

> This foreign gentleman, rich and elderly, who died in a small hotel room, had, with his sister and his two daughters, left Scotland, his country house and his estates and comfortable rural life, to come to our small town and do good among us, to establish a charity and devote to it his time, nights as well as days, his wealth, his health and finally his life.

Sir Hugh Munro is buried in a modest, private graveyard on a peaceful patch of ground hemmed in between a farm hedge and a high garden wall. It is located a short distance west of Drumleys, the family house three miles south of Kirriemuir. His mother and his wife are also buried in this quiet spot.

The fact that Munro died while in the service of others is a sign of his true compassion. That he spent much of his life tramping the Scottish hills in all weathers to climb and classify the summits is a sign of his tenacity and enthusiasm. When he died he was in the process of reclassifying the list of mountains and Tops, and so we will never know for sure quite what he would have altered. One thing is sure, however: the marvellous legacy of Munros and their ascent has developed into something that even Sir Hugh himself could not have envisaged. Munro, one of the original benefactors of the SMC, gave a solid basis not only to the club's subsequent growth but also, much more than that, to the growth of one of the most popular outdoor activities in Scotland today.

CHAPTER 2

The First Munroist

The campaign has been a desultory one, and has occupied about ten years. It was begun with no thought of ever climbing them all, but simply from a desire to obtain a general knowledge of the Highland hills.

A.E. Robertson

History was made on 28 September 1901. The Revd Archibald E. Robertson became the first person to complete all the Munros when he arrived at the Meall Dearg cairn on the celebrated Aonach Eagach of Glencoe. As he did so, it was amusingly recorded by his friend Alexander Moncrieff that he kissed both the cairn and his wife – in that order!

The Revd A.E. Robertson

Robertson had taken a little over ten years to climb the 283 Munros on the original list; a quite incredible feat for the time, considering the lack of good tarred roads, cars and railways – luxuries we now all take for granted. Even with these aids to access, the average completion time for today's Munroist is still around ten years.

Like Munro and almost all climbers of the time, however, Robertson came from a privileged upper-class background where much leisure time was available for lengthy expeditions into the hills. The down-trodden working classes had hardly time to think of Munros, let alone climb them, and it wasn't until the Thirties that this section of society began to make their mark. The advantage of a Rannoch parish and the good fortune of circumstances which allowed him a three-month holiday in 1898 enabled Robertson to add 75 Munros to his list. Another three-month sortie during the following year gave him 72 more.

Robertson was born in Helensburgh in 1870 and his love of the hills was apparent even at the age of 12 when he climbed Goat Fell on Arran alone. After leaving Glasgow Academy, he did not immediately begin a Divinity course but attended Lord Kelvin's class in Natural Philosophy (physics) at the University of Glasgow. Some years later he managed to obtain, with Lord Kelvin's help, a special aneroid barometer for checking the heights of the Scottish hills, and this accompanied him on every climb.

After completing his B.D. course at Edinburgh, he entered the ministry of the Church of Scotland and was assistant at Edinburgh before being ordained to Rannoch in 1907. Unlike Munro, who was a widower for most of his life, Robertson was twice happily married, climbing many Munros with his first wife, Kate, before her death in the mid-Thirties. The second Mrs Robertson (Winnifred) also enjoyed a day out on the hill.

Although Robertson was certainly a Munro-bagger he did possess 'Ultramontane' tendencies and was not scared of technical difficulty. He accomplished some fine rock climbs, including routes on Ben Nevis, Buachaille Etive Mor and the Cobbler. He only had one season in the Alps, but he managed to ascend the Matterhorn and the Rimpfischhorn, commenting that he still preferred his 'good, sound Scottish snow', on which he was also very much an expert.

Robertson was another very influential member of the Scottish Mountaineering Club, and, not surprisingly, armed with much new knowledge and personal experiences, he made many contributions to the *Journal*. His 'Mountain Memories' (volume 24) contains many interesting

1906 SMC meet at the Clachaig Inn, Glencoe, showing some of AER's contemporaries

excerpts from the climbing diaries of his most energetic years, beginning with his lone scramble up Goat Fell on Arran in 1882 and ending with his last Munro in 1901. The best-known article is probably 'The Munros of Scotland' (volume 7), published a year after his completion, which beautifully sums up his 'desultory campaign'.

Like Munro, he had a passionate love of the Scottish hills and enjoyed multi-day jaunts into remote country, using the shelter provided by keepers' and stalkers' cottages. From all accounts, however, he was more discriminating than Munro, and the dirty rooms of Skiary at Loch Hourn where Munro had stayed were politely turned down. The lack of beer or whisky was no doubt also a significant factor! In 'The Munros of Scotland', Robertson strikingly sums up the charms of long mountain trips:

> What delightful weeks I have spent in this manner. The long, fine spring and early summer days, the loneliness and the wonder of the wild and unknown country; no trains, no coaches, no villas, far out of the track of that baneful and vulgar modern product the guide-book tourist. You set forth to traverse your peak, and the only house within 15 miles is that keeper's there, where you must be put up for the night. You sight it with your glass as you lie away up among the tops far down in the glen below. Towards evening you approach the house not without apprehension, the dogs rush out barking vociferously, half in welcome, half in anger. You knock at the door, there is a parley. You are admitted, and once admitted, treated with all the courtesy, dignity and hospitality that are the prime characteristics of the Celtic nature. In all my wanderings I have never been refused a night's shelter.

The exceptional warmth and conviviality of these isolated Highland folk must have been a significant factor in the success of Robertson's many ventures. On his long wilderness trips he depended on these people, lightweight tents and bothying being a thing of the future. Indeed, many of the remote cottages where he stayed with their gracious occupants are now bothies – simple unlocked shelters used by today's hillgoers. One such shelter is Ben Alder Cottage where he stayed with the McCooks on many occasions. Although it was at one time rumoured to be haunted by the ghost of McCook, who was said to have hung himself from a meat hook suspended from the ceiling, the myth of the suicide was thoroughly overturned by a subsequent note in the *SMC Journal*.

Highland hospitality as described by Robertson still exists today in pockets but it must be remembered that 100 years ago the remote glens were far more densely populated than now, with hardy people who were no doubt glad of the odd visitor to their lonely outposts. It is understandable today, with the onslaught of large, colourful and noisy groups of hillwalkers, climbers and mountain-bikers, that the same hospitality is not quite so forthcoming.

Robertson's description of his many hosts is not that of simple rustic folk but of 'well read, well informed, interested, capable and God-fearing' people. He describes one family in which 'the eldest girl, of 14 years of age, had never seen a church or a school in her life, yet for all that; quick witted, intelligent, far more truly *educated* by nature and the occasional visit of a peripatetic teacher than the many town sparrows, crammed with superficial smatterings in our city Board Schools.'

It is also obvious from Robertson's writings that he was not only granted lodgings for the night but given a good square meal as well. Yet again it must be realised that the days of lightweight stoves and pre-packaged or dehydrated foods were a long way off. Nevertheless, Robertson's rucksack was relatively light when compared to that of today's average weekend backpacker. Apart from a heavy cape, binoculars and possibly aneroid barometer, his only other possessions were some evening clothing (including slippers) for use in the numerous dwelling houses. It is interesting to note that he did not take up photography until two years after his completion of the Munros, otherwise a good 10 to 20 pounds in weight would have been added to the above list. For those of us who slip an almost weightless compact camera into the side pocket of a rucksack, it is difficult to imagine lugging round a heavy whole plate camera, wooden tripod legs and fragile glass plates, not to mention the additional complexities of actually setting up the equipment and taking the photograph. Nevertheless, despite these hardships, Robertson became quite an accomplished photographer and many of his pictures appeared in the *SMC Journal*.

Oddly enough, although Munro and Robertson were contemporaries and had similar interests and aspirations, there are no accounts of them joining forces on hill expeditions, even on club meets. It is apparent, however, that both men were strongly independent and unquestionably able to tackle long multi-day Munro-bagging jaunts without the need for any moral support. Indeed, by all accounts both preferred their own company. Apart from these two, no one else at the time appeared to be attempting completion of the Munros and perhaps they saw each other as rivals in a common quest.

Robertson made efficient use of a bicycle on many occasions to reach some of the more remote hills, and could be said to be the first mountain-biker! Since Robertson's time, bikes have been used on numerous occasions to give easier access to isolated peaks. Today's almost maniacal mountain-biking fad is a monstrous mutant of these humble beginnings.

There were, of course, many regions where bicycle or pony-trap could not enter, such as Glen Dessary, Loch Hourn and the more remote parts of

Strathmore Cottage, West Monar, where Robertson found excellent accommodation. The Munros of Sgurr Choinnich and Sgurr a'Chaorachain form the skyline ridge. Sadly, this view no longer exists: the house was occupied by a shepherd until flooded by Loch Monar in 1962 – the watery grave of many Highland dwellings

Kintail, and in 1895 Robertson, together with his two friends Moncrieff and Mirylees, made their first exploratory steps into this wild area. During an Easter meet at the Alexandra Hotel in Fort William they made use of the Arisaig mail coach which left at 8 a.m. and deposited them at Glenfinnan three hours later. From there they tramped up Glen Finnan to the shepherd's cottage of Corryhully (now a bothy) before striking up the south-west shoulder of Sgurr Thuilm. A 'capital glissade' of some 500 feet was secured and they subsequently descended further to the head of Loch Arkaig, where they asked for and obtained accommodation at the large farmhouse at Glen Dessary – still occupied today.

The following morning they continued along the wild and rugged through-route of Glen Dessary, still just as wild today, though somewhat spoiled by forestation on the south side of the glen. The sharp rocky profile of Sgurr na 'h-Aide (a Corbett) attracted them so much that they decided to climb it. Their expectations of some scrambling towards the top were fulfilled – this peak is one of many fine Corbetts in the area. A rugged descent took them to the top of the pass, the Mam na Cloich' Airde, famous in the days of the '45 and Bonnie Prince Charlie. From there they made their way to the head of Loch Nevis, where the present Sourlies Bothy is situated, though no mention was made of this building in Robertson's account. Their accommodation that night was the keeper's cottage at Carnach (now sadly a ruin), where they were duly impressed by his hospitality and kindness.

The next day they ascended the elegantly pointed spire of Sgurr na Ciche, one of the finest Munros in this area and indeed in the whole of Scotland. The views from the summit are magnificent, though on this particular day they were unfortunate with the weather, as Robertson comments:

> A thick mist was driving over the summit, and at this point things looked formidable. Steep pitches of rock were distorted by the vapour into frowning precipices; but as we pierced the veil the face resolved itself into nothing worse than a sharp series of steps and stairs.

Being reassured on the summit by the sight of a dry-stone wall, they gladly followed it and made a quick descent 'by a succession of elongated goat-bounds' into the lonely Coire nan Gall lying to the north-east of the mountain. Five miles further on they reached the keeper's house at Kinlochquoich, now drowned out by the post-war, new and larger version of Loch Quoich. There they were once again shown ample hospitality.

AER and friends climbing in Horse Corrie, Glen Shiel

From Quoich Bridge they headed north the following day to Alltbeithe and crossed the multi-Munroed South Cluanie ridge via Bealach Dubh Leac. A steep descent took them to the 'main road' in Glen Shiel and from there to Shiel Inn, where they had a rather indifferent night.

Part of the Five Sisters ridge was tackled the next day in misty conditions and after a day's rest they resumed operations on Ben Attow (Beinn Fhada), which was at the time locally believed to be one of the highest hills in the Highlands. They then proceeded to Cluanie Bridge, where they found 'a quite admirable little inn of the simplest and most comfortable type'. This is well known now as the much-enlarged Cluanie Inn, a haven for Munro-baggers as it is literally surrounded on all sides by 3,000-foot peaks. At least 20 Munros can be climbed in a few days using the Cluanie Inn as a base.

This is exactly what Robertson & co. did, although they did not quite manage the full 20, and after two or three days they tramped up the glen to Shiel. From there they crossed the Bealach Ratagan to Glenelg, where they caught a homeward-bound steamer.

The Cluanie Inn, Easter 1931. Part of the South Cluanie Ridge forms the imposing skyline

This ten-day jaunt was typical of Robertson's lengthy excursions into the remoter regions of the Highlands. The experience and new knowledge he gleaned on such trips, together with his interest in Highland history, resulted in the publication of a pamphlet *Old Tracks and Cross-Country Routes of the North-West Highlands*. He reached a position of high office in the Royal Scottish Geographical Society and was president of the SMC from 1930 to 1932. He was also closely associated with the Scottish Rights-of-Way Society, becoming a director in 1923, chairman in 1931 and, after reorganisation, its first president in 1946. The Scottish Rights-of-Way Society has built a bridge over the River Elchaig on the way to the Falls of Glomach as a memorial to Robertson.

In his article 'The Munros of Scotland' Robertson writes:

> The first thought that strikes one on looking back over the hills of Scotland as a whole is that there are almost none that have not some fairly easy route to the top – and I regret to say it. For although the most incorrigible of peak-baggers, I love a climb as well. Like the keeper I once asked if he would have a dram or a pint of beer, I most emphatically reply, 'Both is best'! I only wish I could tell the club of some far-away unknown peak bristling with difficulties on all sides, but the fact is there are none. The only hills where there are no easy ways to the top are certain of the Coolins in Skye, Sgurr Dubh for example or Mhadaidh and perhaps Sgurr Alasdair, though on Alasdair you have got the Stone Shoot which leads to within 125 feet of the top.

This extract expresses a general truism about Scottish hills – that the easiest routes to the top possess no real technical difficulties. But many readers who have struggled in apprehension up the exposed edge of the hardest Munro in Scotland will now be asking, 'Yes, but what about the In. Pin.?' If any peak in Scotland is 'bristling with difficulties on all sides' then surely it is the Inaccessible Pinnacle? Yet Robertson makes no mention of it in the above passage, giving the distinct impression that he had not climbed it prior to 1901 when he claimed completion. In fact his own notebooks mention climbing Sgurr Dearg (on which the Inaccessible Pinnacle stands) but no mention is made of the Pinnacle. So are we to conclude that Robertson was not in fact the first Munroist?

The solution to this intriguing riddle is of course that the Pinnacle was inexplicably not given full Munro status by Sir Hugh in the original Tables, as mentioned in Chapter 1. The smaller height of Sgurr Dearg was the Munro, while the In. Pin. was a mere Top. It is still strange, however, that Robertson, with his obvious climbing abilities, did not appear to have attempted the Pinnacle until 1906 when he returned to the Cuillin.

One final note querying Robertson's completion is mentioned by Robin Campbell in the 1989 *SMC Journal*, and concerns Ben Wyvis. On consultation of Robertson's notebooks, it was noted that there was a tick placed by all 283 Munros on the original list, except for Ben Wyvis. Robertson had visited this Munro on an early occasion and 'followed the usual way up, but near the top it came on heavy rain and as I did not want to get soaked, I turned'. Other unfinished peaks were also mentioned but these were returned to on later dates and subsequently acknowledged in his notebooks. No such acknowledgment was ever made for Ben Wyvis.

A youthful and relaxed AER in Skye, 1899. Note the tacketty boots and hemp rope. This is an unusually laid-back image for the time

Robertson was a perfectionist in everything he undertook and it seems doubtful in retrospect that he failed to make the ascent of Ben Wyvis. Yet whether he did or didn't is slightly academic now and he will always be historically recorded as the first Munroist. What really matters was his great love of the Scottish mountains in their many moods, and it is fitting to end this chapter with Robertson's own words:

In conclusion, let me say that I look back upon the days I have spent in pursuing this quest as among the best-spent days of my life. Amid the strange beauty and wild grandeur of rock face and snow slope, scaling Tops where literally almost foot hath never aforetime trod, I have indeed come face to face with the sacred sanctities of Nature, and he would be indeed dull of heart who could see her beauties thus unfolded, feel her hand on his brow, her breath on his cheek, who could see and feel that unmoved. When I call to mind the cast-iron peaks of the Black Coolins, the ridges on Ben Nevis, the gullies on the Buachaille, the rich and varied hues of the Lochinver and Assynt hills, the sea-scapes from the Torridons, the wild, lonely, rolling uplands of the Mam Soul range, or the region in and around Ben Alder – the memory of these things is a priceless possession.

CHAPTER 3

The Birth of the Great Outdoors

Something of value is on the roads and hills, and thousands set out each Saturday to find it.

Alastair Borthwick, *Always a Little Further*

After the Revd A.E. Robertson's completion in 1901 a quite incredible 22 years passed before anyone climbed all the Munros again. Of course, the turmoil of the Great War was the overriding cause, but it is strange that no one responded to the challenge between 1901 and 1914. Perhaps Robertson's successors wanted to find new challenges. This is exactly what the second Munroist, the Revd A.R.A. Burn, did – he not only climbed the Munros but added the subsidiary Tops as well, a total of over 500 summits. It is curiously interesting that the first two Munroists were men of the cloth. Perhaps this is a divine indication that climbing Munros is a religious and reverential pursuit, pursued only by the devout! Judging by the fanatical devotion to their aim of many of today's Munro-baggers, this statement isn't far from the truth.

Six years later, in 1929, the third Munroist, J.A. Parker, not only climbed the Munros but this time went on to include all the 3,000-foot peaks in England, Wales and Ireland, an addition which has come to be known as the 'Furth of Scotland'. Many people erroneously refer to the 'English Munros' or the 'Welsh Munros', possibly more as a convenience rather than a deliberate error. The term 'Munro' for a 3,000-foot summit can logically only be applied in Scotland as Hugh Munro did not classify the 'Furth of Scotland'. Not surprisingly, the demands of the purists have resulted in a classification of these 3,000-foot peaks into 'mountains' and 'Tops'. By general consensus, England has four 'mountains', Wales eight and Ireland seven, though this classification certainly does not bear the same 'official stamp' as the Scottish Munros. Surprisingly, the 'grand slam' of Munros *and* Tops *and* Furth of Scotland did not fall until as late as 1949, when they were completed by Willie Docharty (Munroist number 13).

J. Rooke Corbett became the fourth Munroist in 1930 and, not to be outdone by Hugh Munro, decided to make his own list of 2,500-foot mountains in Scotland. He subsequently climbed them all and today they are known as 'Corbetts'. Corbett's classification was more rigid and well-defined than Munro's rather subjective observations – he defined a 'Corbett' as a hill 2,500 feet or over but having also a drop of 500 feet or more from any adjacent higher hill. This restriction ensures that Corbetts are more distinct hills than Munros and there are also less of them – 221 to be exact. Corbetts have not reached the almost cult status of Munros but many 'compleat' Munroists are finding that they are a challenging fresh stimulus to wandering feet. (For more about Corbett and his hills see Chapter 9.)

In his article 'The Munros of Scotland', A.E. Robertson opens with the words 'Peak-bagging and record-breaking are somewhat, I fear, looked down upon by the members of the SMC. And outside of the Club they are as a rule regarded in the same unfavourable light.' This observation reflects the rift between Salvationist and Ultramontane members of the club, the latter being 'hard men' or technical climbers and probably in the majority at the time. W.W. Naismith, the founder of the SMC, was one such person and many of his early rock-climbing discoveries have now reached 'classic-route' status. It is interesting, however, that his name will be forever linked with the now-famous hillwalking rule for calculating the time required for a day on the hill. 'Naismith's Rule' gives an hour for every three miles, plus half an hour for every 1,000 feet of ascent. This tried and tested formula forms the basis of most guide-book calculations today.

Other distinguished Ultramontanes of the time included men such as Raeburn, Collie, Glover and Ling whose prolific achievements could fill a book. Perhaps the most notable achievement of the time was the first traverse of the Cuillin Ridge in Skye on 10 June 1911 by L.G. Shadbolt and A.C. McLaren. Considered by many leading lights of the day to be virtually impossible, it is regularly completed today, although this still does not detract from its description as the finest mountaineering expedition in Britain.

The main Cuillin Ridge in the purest sense contains nine Munros, but oddly enough this does not include Sgurr Alasdair, the highest peak 'on the ridge'. The inverted commas signify the fact that Sgurr Alasdair lies just off the main ridge, though by such a small amount that in any traverse it would be churlish not to include it. Sgurr Dubh Mor, on the other hand, lies some way off the ridge and involves a fair bit of descent and re-ascent. Being a Munro, it is often included in any traverse but involves a significant detour. It was not included in the first traverse in 1911.

In his article for the *SMC Journal* Shadbolt opens with the following lines: 'In common with, I suppose, most people who have climbed in the Cuillins, I have always looked with longing eyes at the great stretch of

The Cuillin of
Skye: on Collie's
Ledge of Sgurr
Mhic Choinnich

narrow summit ridge, and speculated on the possibility of making a
continuous climb along it from end to end in one day.' At 3.30 on the
morning of 10 June 1911 these 'dreams of the winter fireside' were about to
enter the 'realms of accomplished action'. Shadbolt and McLaren reached
the summit of Garsbheinn at 6 a.m. after a two-and-a-half-hour walk from
Glen Brittle – they were already one-and-a-half hours ahead of schedule.
By the time they reached Sgurr Dearg they had made at least another hour
and 'the moral effect of being ahead of schedule time was excellent; pipes
were lit, and the sense of having to hurry altogether lost, not, I think, to the
detriment of speed, but certainly to the great enhancement of the
enjoyment of the day'.

The fact that early morning mist had now cleared to give almost
cloudless skies and a gentle wind was a further boost to the determined pair
and the next few hours were probably the most enjoyable of the day as
Shadbolt narrates:

Over Sgurr na Banachdich, Sgurr Thormaid, and Sgurr a' Ghreadaidh
one experienced to the full the delight of striding along narrow ridges
almost unhindered by problems as to the best route, and able to enjoy to
the full the aesthetic side of mountaineering, the true appreciation of
which is, to my mind, only reached in conjunction with sustained
physical effort to the limit of one's powers.

At 6.25 p.m. they stood on the shapely spire of Sgurr nan Gillean, the last Munro on the ridge, and Shadbolt and McLaren entered the mountaineering history books. They had spent just over 12 hours on the ridge; today's Cuillin-ridge record stands at an awesome three hours 32 minutes (see Chapter 5). Sligachan was reached at 8.20 p.m. but before then, in the words of Shadbolt, 'we had thrilled again to all the delights and doubts of one of the best days we had ever spent together on the hills'.

Shadbolt and McLaren had proved beyond doubt that the Cuillin Ridge traverse was within the capabilities of many climbers, yet it is strange that no repeat performance was made until 1920. Again the First World War was probably partly to blame.

No mention of women has yet been made in this historical background and it would be fair to say that opportunities for women to go off into the hills and do their thing were severely limited. The SMC of the early part of this century was a male-dominated brotherhood with a sexist tradition seemingly incorporated into its very foundations, and it is only very recently that women were finally admitted. Any women who were independent and liberated enough to indulge in the 'manly sport' of mountaineering were looked on as strangely eccentric. However, in the spring of 1908 in the appropriate setting of the lee of a large boulder near Killin, the Ladies' Scottish Climbing Club was formed. This memorable event had followed a spell of spring mountaineering on the surrounding hills. It is somewhat amusing to study old photographs of women climbers in billowing skirts and enormous hats with motoring veils, which must have transformed any hill walk or rock climb into an extremely taxing affair. It is not surprising that many of the wearers abandoned their costumes once they were safely hidden from prying eyes. The activities of these early 'climbing Suffragettes' were a moral backlash against an incorrigible upper-class set of male egotists. Although the women of the time never reached the dizzy mountaineering heights of their male counterparts, they had at least gained a foothold in a male-dominated scene.

By the dawning of the depressed Thirties another sphere of humanity was to make its timely and refreshingly couthy contribution to the mountaineering world. As the dole queues lengthened in the streets and the jobless total topped three million, thousands of working-class folk escaped the soul-destroying vacuum of unemployment and looked to the hills for fresh inspiration and challenge in their bleak lives. In Glasgow the once proud and world-famous shipbuilding industry on Clydeside was at a complete standstill and throughout central Scotland unemployment was rampant. In England too, in cities such as Sheffield and Manchester, hordes of disillusioned unemployed folk escaped their back-to-back existence in drab terraces and hopped on a bus to the misty moorland charms of the Peak District.

The Beinn Narnain 'Howff'. Alastair Borthwick's brother, Jim, is sitting to the right (facing picture) of the man with the 'mouthie'

Glasgow had the compensation of being only a stone's throw from the delights of the Campsies, Trossachs, Luss hills and 'Arrochar Alps'. The latter group not only contained a handful of Munros but also one of the best rock-climbing peaks in the Southern Highlands – the Cobbler. This was the mecca for hardened Glasgow climbers of the time and supports scores of routes on its three conspicuous peaks.

Yet the exploration of new routes and the joys of peak-bagging were not the only activities which these rugged individuals indulged in. The circumstances of the time forced the majority to sleep rough in barns, ruined cottages, caves and that most ubiquitous of habitats the 'howff'. A howff was a natural rock shelter (or possibly a cave) which was subsequently subjected to much human alteration and improvement. Many of the huge boulders underneath the Cobbler made ideal howffs and on a summer evening in the Thirties it would be no surprise to find them all occupied.

Perhaps the most respected and experienced 'howffer' of the time was the late Ben Humble, who wrote:

> Mountain camping is all very well, but the inside of a tent is always the same and once in there is nothing to do. Each howff is different, each has its building problems, each its own charm, each its own memories. And there is always so much to do, for howffing refinements are endless.

Nor was howffing restricted to summer-time. Ben Humble had always 'hankered for a cave under real winter conditions', and he found it one Hogmanay in the Lost Valley of Glencoe:

My brightest memory is of sallying forth in the deep snow, returning with two armfuls of icicles and discovering that porridge made from icicles was much better than porridge made from snow. Conditions that night had been just about as severe as could be experienced in Scotland.

Ben Humble's regular howffing and climbing companion was Jock Nimlin, a superb rock-climber. He, too, exalted in the spartan charms of howffing and he talks of his experiences at the Shelter Stone, a famous howff in the Cairngorms:

On the New Year of 1936, when I had cut down load-carrying to the exclusion of sleeping-bag, five of us slept at the Shelter Stone of Loch Avon in the sub-zero temperature. With two men on either side encased in eiderdown bags, I slept in coat and sweaters, with feet stuffed into a rucksack. True, my teeth were chattering when I wakened, but I had enjoyed eight hours' sleep, and four other sets of teeth were chattering in unison . . .

It must be noted that eiderdown sleeping-bags – indeed any kind of sleeping-bags – were only for the few. Most didn't even carry a blanket, and

Alltbeithe Youth Hostel in Glen Affric. Ciste Dhubh is in the background

newspapers were the norm. For these hardy souls there was little alternative to living rough, and the luxury of a soft bed and a roof over their head was something they simply could not afford. Even the cost of a tent was prohibitive to many climbers and walkers.

An event took place in Edinburgh on 13 February 1931 which was to add further momentum to the Great Outdoor revolution and which was primarily aimed at the younger set. An organisation was formed whose main objective was:

> To help all, but especially young people of limited means living and working in industrial and other areas to know, use and appreciate the Scottish Countryside and places of historic and cultural interest in Scotland and to promote their health, recreation and education, particularly by providing simple hostel accommodation for them on their travels.

The organisation was the Scottish Youth Hostels Association, which today is a flourishing business. Some of the more remote hostels are ideal bases for exploring Scotland's wildest country and, of course, for Munro-climbing. Hostels such as Alltbeithe in Glen Affric, Loch Ossian and Glendoll are hemmed in by 3,000-foot peaks.

It should be stressed, however, that for many of the howffing 'hard men' from the industrial heartlands, youth hostels were seen as too militaristic and institutionalised – and besides they were a shilling a night. Lights out at 11 o'clock was certainly not for those who revelled in the atmosphere of a candle-lit howff, enjoying the 'crack' and camaraderie of like-minded souls. Howffs also had the distinct advantage of being on the hill and only a stone's throw away from the best rock climbs.

The true atmosphere and character of these heady pre-war days is perhaps no more brilliantly portrayed than in Alastair Borthwick's classic piece of mountaineering literature *Always a Little Further*. First published in 1939, it has by popular demand had three re-publications, the most recent by Diadem in 1989. It is, as the subtitle tells us, 'a classic tale of camping, hiking and climbing in Scotland in the Thirties'. It is also a precious store of colourful characters, earthy humour and utterly engaging anecdotes and exploits. It could be called a period piece, but its fundamental honesty and inoffensiveness ultimately make it a timeless masterpiece.

One chapter describes the author's first trip to Skye, in 1933 – a memorable experience for anyone, but it became almost a test of survival for Alastair and his three companions. In those days the boat from Mallaig sailed to Broadford (not Armadale), and the four, having reached Broadford at 4 p.m., were told that the bus had departed and that the next one wasn't due until 9 p.m. A hasty decision was made to attempt to walk the 30 miles to Glen Brittle, most of it cross-country. They made 12 miles that night on an empty stomach and an empty road and pitched the tent where they were due to start their cross-country section. After eating what few sandwiches they had, a miserably cold night was spent before rising at 4 a.m. and heading for what they took to be a village at the remote spot of Camasunary. By six o'clock it was beginning to get light and desperation and depression had descended over the party when suddenly they 'stopped dead in their tracks and gaped'.

> The whole vast chain of the Black Cuillin, from Gars-bheinn to Sgurr nan Gillean, was stretched out like a curtain before us, with the sun, which had not yet dropped to our level, lighting the range from end to end. The mountains seemed close enough to touch. The morning mist was rising from them, softly, effortlessly, revealing first one buttress, then another, of the 20 peaks which stretched for miles, linked into a continuous whole by high ridges, scored by gullies, turreted, pinnacled, heaved up to the sky; rock, rock and more rock as far as the eye could see. And, Black Cuillin or not, they were blue, the pale, delicate blue of a spring sunset, matt like a butterfly's wing. As the mist dissolved, more and more peaks took the skyline, more and more pinnacles broke the ridges, until only the gullies smoked. Then the last puff dissolved and broke, and they, too, were clear. The Cuillin were ours.

Shadbolt's observation that a true appreciation of mountain beauty is only fully reached in conjunction with sustained physical effort seems absolutely inherent in this immortal passage of Borthwick's. What glorious imagery this passage conveys, and what a memorable first impression the four had of the Cuillin ridge; made all the more memorable by the effort they had expended to experience it. A first glimpse of the Cuillin through a car window just doesn't have the same impact.

However, the raised spirits of the by-now-ravenous four were soon to be cruelly dampened when they reached the 'village' of Camasunary, to find only one unoccupied house. Their dreams of ham and eggs remained just that, and the only nourishment they found was a few brambles on the shores of Loch Scavaig. After discovering that Borthwick had dropped the tent-pegs on crossing the Bad Step, they spent another night in the open, tentless, but ironically warmer, as heather had been piled several feet deep to form insulation from the ground.

The following day was a gruelling 'hunger march', since the party had eaten their last hot meal over 48 hours ago. As Borthwick relates: 'Hunger, we discovered, was not the localised pain we had imagined it to be . . . We were hungry all over. Our finger-tips were hungry.'

Yet despite the hunger, the heat and the weakness of their exhausted bodies, Borthwick remembers resting below Corrie Lagan and gazing up at the highest peak in the Cuillin, Sgurr Alasdair:

> The sky was clear blue and cloudless, so that the final razor-edge of the ridge below the summit was thrown up in sharp relief. And as I watched I saw four tiny figures crawl out on to the skyline and scramble slowly to the top. I was excited. I was tired and thirsty, and hungry; but I still had it in me to be excited. We hoped to be up there soon.

Indeed, a day or two later, after some well-deserved rest and food, they did venture up on to the ridge after consulting their more experienced mentor, Hamish, as to a suitable climb. His advice was short but beautifully to the point:

> Well, it's like this. There are five classes of climbs in Skye – easy, moderate, difficult, very difficult, and severe. Easy is a walk. Moderate isn't much better. When you land on a difficult, you're getting somewhere. If *you* land on a very difficult, you won't get anywhere. And if you see a severe, raise your hat and walk past it.

Hamish concluded by recommending that they attempt the Window Buttress of Sgurr Dearg, 'a nice easy-ish difficult'. On reaching the summit of Sgurr Dearg, he informed them of the Inaccessible Pinnacle and how the west side was 'not for little boys' – the east side was the easier route. After bungling their way up Window Buttress they reached the In. Pin. in dense mist and were at a loss in deciding whether the steep ridge they were facing was the east or west ridge. They wrongly supposed it to be the easier east ridge but nevertheless made it to the top after quite a struggle.

The descent proved to be even more difficult as the blundering four were ignorant of abseiling techniques. As Borthwick was attempting to unjam a rope from an awkward position halfway down the pinnacle, the others were raving about the beautiful sunset, which proved, as one of them pointed out, that they had in fact ascended and descended the west, most difficult side of the Pinnacle.

Another classic book of the time which captures to perfection the innocence and youthful enthusiasm of climbing in the Thirties is Tom Weir's *Highland Days*. Like Borthwick's *Always a Little Further*, it has had several re-publications and has deservedly become a minor classic.

Tom Weir was born in Springburn in Glasgow in 1914 and belonged to the first generation of working-class outdoor men. Springburn is one of

Tom Weir (left) and his companion Matt Forrester on the hills in 1933

the highest parts of Glasgow and Tom remembers vividly his first childhood view of sparkling white peaks beckoning tantalisingly on the horizon to the north, set against a clear blue sky. This stirred within him a passion for wild places and nature which was to last a lifetime and subsequently to earn him a living into the bargain. He has written numerous books and literally thousands of articles, contributing regularly to the *Scots Magazine*. His TV series *Weir's Way* won him the STV Personality of the Year Award in 1978 and continues to be watched by record numbers.

Tom Weir's sheer love and enthusiasm for the outdoors shines through in all of his writing and he writes with a freshness and sensitivity which never flags. He not only enjoys the scenery of Scotland but has a keen and observant eye for wildlife and natural history. One quote from *Highland Days* captures the mood of a summer evening in Glen Brittle on Skye with effortless precision:

> Later the moon rose, sending a lane of silver across the water. From the gabbro sands came sounds I grew to love, the shrill pipings of mingled oyster-catchers and redshanks. At our backs wedged against the dark sky were the peaks, sliced cleaner and sharper than we had ever seen before.

This was written on Weir's first visit to the Cuillin, in 1933 when he was only 18 – the same year that Alastair Borthwick and his cronies also saw the Cuillin for the first time. The story of his exploits contains interesting parallels to Borthwick's hunger march, described in Chapter 3 of *Highland Days*.

Weir's early outdoor wanderings encompassed a whole spectrum of activities from rock-climbing to bird-watching to Munro-bagging. A mixed bag of weather accompanied him on one particular peak-bagging foray to Glen Cannich, one of the 'central glens' of Affric, Cannich and Strathfarrar which contain a 'rich harvest' of Munros. After a misty start on the Munros of Beinn Fhionnlaidh and Carn Eighe, he describes his joy as the mist cleared *en route* to Mam Sodhail:

> . . . as I left the top the clouds broke open. Blue peaks leapt out of the north and south. With a thrill I recognised the spire of Liathach and the Torridon mountains. Sgorr na Ciche of Knoydart, another old friend, was unmistakably recognisable, and I could see the sunshine on Ben Nevis, the scoring of its cliffs quite visible. I was massed round with ridges and tangled up in peaks and deep glens, a bewildering effect as the mist flirted with this new mountainland of mine.

By the time war broke out in 1939, Weir had climbed 306 Tops, as he notes by the ticks in his Munro's Tables – not bad for someone who was only 25 at the time.

This brief survey of Thirties mountaineering literature would not be complete without mentioning another classic – *Mountaineering in Scotland* by W.H. Murray. The book is available today along with *Undiscovered Scotland*, published as a single volume by Diadem. It was written during the war in prison-of-war camps and is a vivid and highly descriptive

Tom Weir, still active on the hills today

recollection of the author's climbing experiences from his commencement in 1934 to the outbreak of war.

Like many other of his contemporaries, W.H. Murray's first mountain experience was on the Cobbler. He had gone in ordinary street clothes: shirt, tie and normal shoes. Hard frozen snow in the corrie did not stop him kicking steps and reaching the top of the centre peak. He then continued along the ridge and climbed 'walls of sun-washed rock' to the south peak. In his innocence he had committed many sins of mountaineering. He had climbed steep snow slopes in street clothes with no boots, ice-axe, map, compass, protective clothing or companions. He describes his feelings on reaching the top:

> I looked out upon the mountains circling me in a white-topped throng, and receding to horizons that rippled against the sky like a wash of foam. Not one of these hills did I know by name, and every one was probably as worth exploring as the Cobbler . . . From that day I became a mountaineer.

Bill Murray

On returning home and consulting books, he learned that there are 543 mountain-tops in Scotland over 3,000 feet. This fact filled him with frustration as the idea that anyone could climb them all did not seem possible. He then spent a year darting round Scotland, 'snatching mountains here, there, and everywhere', still alone as he was unable to find any companions. In 1935 he joined the Junior Mountaineering Club of Scotland and began rock-climbing.

Winter mountaineering was his first love, however, and he was the leading exponent of severe Scottish winter climbing from 1935 to 1939. His preference for winter mountaineering is reflected beautifully in the following extract and echoes the feelings of many mountaineers:

> . . . for it is in winter that the Scottish hills excel. No one who has seen the skyward thrust of a snow peak, girdled by its early morning cloud wisp and flushed with the low sun, will dispute with me. Follow a long ridge of encrusted rock to its sunset tower, tread the summit at moon-rise; and you will agree that without that intense experience your life would have been a poorer thing.

Although W.H. Murray has climbed much since the war, not only in Scotland but also in the Alps and Himalayas, he rates his pre-war years on the Scottish hills as his best – a time when his passion, enthusiasm and physical fitness were all at their peak. This final quote sums up the emotions of those years perfectly, and celebrates stunningly the beauty of the winter scene:

46

The new Glencoe road under construction, May 1930: rock-cutting at the Study

. . . in the worst days of the war there shone most often before my eyes the clear vision of that evening on Nevis, when the snow plateau sparkled red at sunset, and of Glencoe, when the frozen towers of Bidian burned in the moon. In the last resort, it is the beauty of the mountain world in the inmost recesses that holds us spellbound, slaves until life ends.

The Thirties saw a general upsurge in all mountain activities among people of all walks of life. The hikers and bikers, the ramblers and scramblers, and the technical climbers all enjoyed the hills in their own special way. The Youth Hostels Association was a thriving business and the new road to Glencoe opened in 1933. New climbing clubs had formed, such as the Ptarmigan Club, the Craig Dhu and the Lomond Mountaineering Club. It is surprising, therefore, that in spite of all this outdoor escapism only eight people had climbed all the Munros before the Second World War.

Munroist number 5, J. Dow, who completed in 1933, made the point that the ascent of the Munros 'under modern road and transport conditions is very far from being in the slightest degree a feat'. What would he have made of the situation today? He also admits that 'never once did I fail to return to a hot bath and a comfortable bed, and very rarely did I even miss dinner, so that in actual fact the whole affair was in my case pretty much of a luxury progress'. Dow's approach represents the antithesis of the howffing fraternity's principles, and it is obvious that he did not belong to the working class or unemployed masses of the depressed Thirties.

Within weeks of the outbreak of the war another remarkable piece of mountaineering history was made on Skye. Twenty-eight years after Shadbolt and McLaren's epic traverse of the main Cuillin Ridge, the traverse was repeated but this time the outlying Blaven was included. This route is now known as the Greater Traverse. As well as the usual 10,000 feet of climbing, there is a drop to almost sea-level followed by a further 3,000-foot ascent and another tricky traverse of Clach Glas and Blaven. Between first and last summits the feat took 20 hours and was performed by Charleson and Forde in June 1939.

In August 1939 W.H. Murray and R.G. Donaldson amazingly repeated the feat and knocked an hour off the peak-to-peak time. Admittedly, they did have better luck with the weather but had problems navigating their way off Blaven. Their total time from tent to tent was an incredible 27 hours.

A fortnight after Murray and Donaldson's exploit, Britain was at war, and to all intents and purposes recreational mountaineering and hillwalking were repulsed. The trickle of eight pre-war Munroists was temporarily halted in its tracks, but the trickle was poised and ready to burst into a torrential flood in the post-war years.

CHAPTER 4

The Post-War Revolution

No exploit in the mountains ever seems to leave the heart at rest, and the Munros were no exception. The direction, style and location may alter, but a love of wild places and the search for their challenge seems only to be increased by hard experience. Devotion or addiction, call it what you will.

Martin Moran, *The Munros in Winter*

On 23 November 1991 in the Roxburghe Hotel in Edinburgh, 223 people congregated to celebrate a very special occasion. One hundred years had passed since the publication of Hugh Munro's hallowed tables of mountains over 3,000 feet. Of the 223 guests, 155 had completed all the Munros and the majority of the remainder were long-suffering spouses. Yet the 155 Munroists present at the centenary celebration comprised only a fraction of 'compleat' Munroists at the time. In fact, by the end of 1991 it was recorded that over 1,000 people had completed the Munros. The pre-war 'trickle' of eight Munroists had indeed reached torrent proportions, but just what were the circumstances that eventually led to this veritable flood?

Post-war Britain in the late Forties slowly began to recover from the ravages of conflict, and the sense of freedom and new beginning gave fresh impetus to many people. Increased leisure time was an invitation to take up new hobbies and interests, and in particular the Great Outdoors held a fascination for a growing band of devotees. 1947 saw the first post-war completion but was also notable for two other reasons. Mr and Mrs J. Hirst became the first married couple to do all the Munros and Mrs Hirst, at number 10, was the first woman. Another 13 years were to pass before the second female completion, so Munro-bagging was still very much a man's game. By the end of the Forties the Munroist tally had risen to 15 – in the three years since 1947 almost as many people had completed the Munros as had done so in the 38 years prior to the Second World War.

The rapid growth of the outdoor fraternity produced an increased awareness of training and safety, and in 1948 the Scottish Centre of Outdoor

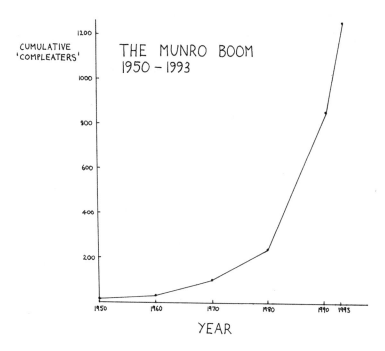

Training was formed at Glenmore Lodge. On 31 July of the same year the first experimental outdoor courses for young people were begun and Glenmore Lodge earned its place in history as the first civilian mountain-training centre in Britain. Today, Glenmore Lodge has become almost synonymous with mountain training and the full spectrum of outdoor activities is taught – from sailing to abseiling, rock-climbing to rescue techniques, summer hillwalking to winter ice-climbing, canoeing to cross-country skiing; the list goes on.

By the Fifties Munro-bagging was steadily gaining popularity and another 20 names were added to the list. One momentous event of the Fifties was to capture the public's imagination and symbolise man's struggle against the elements. On Coronation Day 1953 Edmund Hillary and Sherpa Tenzing reached the summit of Everest. This famous 'first' brought mountains to the public's attention and pursuaded people that climbing them could be fun as well as being a personal challenge. There is no doubt that this historic event sparked off a new wave of enthusiasm and interest in all aspects of mountaineering, including the climbing of Munros.

For the man in the street, Everest was an impossible dream, but the Munros provided a challenge which was not insurmountable – the Munros became his own personal Everest.

The Fifties saw a meteoric rise in the number of families owning a motor car. Together with the rapid improvements of roads in the

Highlands, this made for easy access to previously extremely remote areas. For many former non-hillwalkers, the sight of, say, fresh spring snow glistening on a distant ridge while on a Highland holiday was the vital spark which set them off on years of hill-tramping.

An exponential rise in the number of Munroists was now evident and by 1970 the 100 mark was up. 1961 saw the publication of the first monthly magazine devoted entirely to mountaineering – *Climber and Rambler* (published by George Outram & Co. Ltd). The magazine has gone from strength to strength over the years and today is still one of the bestselling mountaineering periodicals despite fierce competition from a growing selection of rivals. (It is now known as *Climber and Hillwalker*.)

Numerous books about the Highlands and Islands were published soon after the war, but for most people the series of guides published by the Scottish Mountaineering Club provided the essential information they required. The SMC's *General Guide* to the Scottish hills, first published in 1921, was the mountaineer's 'bible' of the time and contained a list of all the

Ben Alder Cottage, a popular and fairly remote MBA bothy

51

Munros at the back. However, it was the type of book which catered for all hill types, including hillwalkers, rock-climbers, snow-and-ice climbers, botanists, geologists and bird-watchers. It was obvious that all these specialist facets could not be comprehensively covered within one book, and inevitably books began to appear which concentrated on specific hill-related disciplines.

In 1965 one such book specifically about hillwalking in Scotland was published and soon became a bestseller. *The Scottish Peaks* by W.A. Poucher (Constable) was described by *Climber and Rambler* magazine as 'nothing less than a monumental work'. The book was a companion volume to Poucher's other British mountain guide-books such as *The Lakeland Peaks* and *The Welsh Peaks*, and has his own special stamp of superb photographs, many with the actual route marked on them. One unique aspect of the book is the inclusion of one-inch-to-the-mile Ordnance Survey map reproductions, which was a major selling point considering the cost of maps. It is a testimony to the book's enormous popularity that despite the competition from scores of glossy, coloured rivals it still has a place in today's hill-walking market. This volume and Poucher's *The Magic of Skye* are undoubtedly his two bestselling books.

An organisation was formed in 1965 whose aim was 'to maintain simple unlocked shelters in remote country for the use of walkers, climbers and other outdoor enthusiasts who love the wild and lonely places'. The Mountain Bothies Association was inaugurated by Bernard Heath when a handful of enthusiasts began renovating a ruined cottage at Tunskeen in the Galloway hills. The project involved an incredible amount of sheer strength and manpower considering that all the materials – including cement and corrugated iron – had to be carried over miles of desolate moorland. The success of the venture was a marvellous encouragement and the work party hit upon the idea of an organisation whose function would be to renovate and maintain old crofts and cottages for the use of outdoor people.

It was realised, of course, that although literally hundreds of deserted 'bothies' lay scattered around Scotland and England's remote hill country, they all effectively belonged to somebody, and the landowner's permission had first to be granted before any renovation could begin. In most cases permission was granted, indeed welcomed with open arms. After all, the landowner was benefiting from the renovation and constant maintenance of a property on his land – free of charge – and he still owned the property, not the MBA. Not only that, but the MBA were an entirely voluntary body whose only source of income was from paid-up members and other generous contributions. The catch inherent in all this was that the landowner was in effect allowing anyone to walk on his land and use his bothy. He was, by his own approval of the MBA's renovation scheme, effectively encouraging greater numbers of people on his land.

In an ideal world the above system would present no problems. The MBA's code of practice requests bothy users to 'respect other users', 'respect the bothy' and 'respect the surroundings'. These are simple enough requests which the majority of outdoor people adhere to. Unfortunately, there will always be a few who leave their mark in the form of vandalism, graffiti and discarded piles of tins and bottles. Even the more remote bothies have not completely escaped the ravages of the common vandal and the issue is causing growing concern. In the MBA newsletter of September 1992 it was mentioned that the Scottish Youth Hostels Association was no longer leaving the remote Alltbeithe Youth Hostel in Glen Affric unlocked during the winter months, due to misuse. It seems even youth hostels are not safe from wilful destruction. The ripping of pine panelling from the walls for use as firewood is an unbelievable act of inexcusable ignorance – but it has happened at Alltbeithe. In the same newsletter it was reported that a group of people staying at Shiel of Glentanar Bothy had left a large fire burning while they climbed Mount Keen (the most easterly Munro) to watch the sunrise – it was mid-summer's day. When they returned, the bothy was completely gutted. Another bothy, Nest of Fannich, was completely gutted in 1990, and more recently Blackburn of Pattack was destroyed in 1993. Admittedly, these were presumably acts of gross negligence and not wilful destruction, but in the end it is bothy destruction caused by a human.

However, it would be churlish to dwell for too long on these negative aspects of the bothying scene. Since the formation of the MBA, countless people have used bothies and discovered that bothying is almost an end in itself. Even if the rain and wind are lashing against the window and the mist is low on the hills, the crack and camaraderie of fellow hillwalkers round a crackling log fire, complete with a good malt, is reason enough to be out in 'the wild and lonely places'.

Finally, it should be mentioned that the MBA has close on 100 bothies in its care throughout Britain, the majority of these in Scotland. Many are extremely well placed for use as a base for climbing some of the more remote groups of Munros. It is not surprising that on a Bank Holiday weekend or an Easter weekend these particular bothies can be choked out and any prospective bothy-dweller must be prepared to camp.

One other major event of 1965 indirectly related to Munros must surely be mentioned before returning to mainstream Munro-bagging. In February of that year the first winter traverse of the Cuillin Ridge was made by the redoubtable Tom Patey and Hamish MacInnes, together with D. Crabbe and B. Robertson. Because of their proximity to warm Atlantic airstreams, the Cuillin seldom come into condition for winter climbing; that is, they seldom carry any snow or ice for any length of time. The combination of a heavy snowfall, no wind, a quick thaw and a sudden freeze are more or less essential if success is to be guaranteed. Also, good weather must last for at least two days as this is the time-span required. Not surprisingly, this unlikely combination of events does not happen very often, and Tom Patey and co. were lucky to be in the right place at the right time in February 1965.

A superb account of the two-day traverse is given in Patey's classic of mountaineering literature *One Man's Mountains* (Gollancz, 1971), in which he remarks that 'the winter traverse of the Main Ridge will always retain its place as the greatest single adventure in British mountaineering'.

Patey's assertion has a rather grandiose finality about it. To borrow from the language of lager advertising, it is perhaps better described as '*probably* the greatest single adventure in British mountaineering'. This laboured observation is, of course, leading on to the pronouncement that an even greater single adventure in British mountaineering exists – no, not the Greater Cuillin Traverse in winter (though that would be quite something), but the traverse of all the Munros in a single expedition. Such was the stuff of dreams in the Sixties. And what about all the Munros in a single expedition in *winter*? This was many steps ahead and almost unthinkable. The crucial point is that whatever one person sees as the ultimate expedition of his or her generation inevitably regresses to the back seat in the next generation. This is not to detract at all from Tom Patey's assertion – in a strictly mountaineering sense, the bold natural line of the Cuillin Ridge in winter presents a clearly defined challenge within the scope of winter climbers, and it only requires two days. A continual climb of all the Munros would require months and would be more suitably described as '(probably!) the greatest single adventure in British *hillwalking*'.

Many long multi-Munro trips did take place in the Sixties, undertaken by RAF Rescue teams who made several east-west and north-south traverses, the longest of these taking in a total of 58 Munros. However, it was not until 1967 that an attempt was made on all the Munros in a single expedition, by two brothers, Brian and Alan Ripley. A relatively unhurried round of the Munros, including rest days, could be expected to take three to four months – weather and other factors permitting. Therefore, an April start would appear to be ideal, thus finishing before the stalking season in August and avoiding the worst of the midges. Yet the Ripley brothers did not *start* until August, which was a crucial handicap both for the reasons given above and because by late October and November inclement weather had to be expected. Thus, their tally of 230 Munros (47 short of completion) was absolutely astounding, and one could safely assume that had they started in April, success would surely have been theirs.

So why the August start? It seems the Ripley brothers were relatively unfamiliar with the Scottish hills, and stalking, midges and bad weather did not rate highly in their pre-expedition planning. It was also apparent that a pressing series of other appointments forced them to start so late in the summer.

The Ripleys' idea of self-propulsion, i.e. no motorised transport (apart from ferries to the islands), was adhered to at the beginning, but gradually eroded as they began to accept lifts and use buses on long road stretches. The combination of heavy packs, blisters, the need to stock up with supplies, persistent bad weather, shorter daylight hours and financial worries soon began to make their mark, and on 10 November on Beinn Dorain they decided to pack it in. It was probably the worst day's weather they had experienced on the entire trip. At the end of the trip, Alan's ankles were considerably swollen and a doctor diagnosed iron deficiencies.

It was not until almost seven years later, on 4 April 1974, that Hamish Brown set off on his three-and-a-half-month Munro marathon which was destined to become a landmark in Munro history, and the subsequent book, *Hamish's Mountain Walk* (Gollancz), a milestone in mountaineering literature. Hamish Brown is today probably the best-known Munroist and with seven separate completions (to date) retains the monopoly on 'poly-Munroism'. Ironically, he does not claim to be a Munro-bagger!

Hamish was formerly on the staff at Braehead School in Fife, where he took charge of outdoor activities and introduced many young people to the joys of the Scottish hills, and Munros in particular. He organised a hillwalking club which required new members to have climbed at least ten Munros. With the closure of the school he became County Adviser on Mountain Activities and seemed destined for a desk-bound job – until one day in his office he spread out a map of Scotland on the floor, and the idea, like a seed, was well and truly sown.

He had already completed three rounds of the Munros, which was something of a record as nobody at that time had done more than two rounds – Philip Tranter was the first to complete his second round as far back as 1964. Hamish was therefore extremely well prepared and knew exactly what he was in for. He had read the Ripley brothers' account and learned from their mistakes, especially the dietary problems and vitamin deficiencies. Many months of planning and organisation preceded the big trek, and in some respects this was harder than the walk itself.

Hamish undertook the walk largely on his own, although he was supported by an indispensable back-up team of friends and relatives who brought supplies, ferried his bicycle and provided occasional moral support and companionship. Apart from the island ferries, no mechanised transport was used other than a folding bicycle for the road sections. Hamish

Hamish Brown, the first person to complete a continuous round of the Munros

recognised the importance of good food and a high calorie intake, and the morale boost that these provide. It is a common misconception among non-backpackers (and even some backpackers) that dehydrated food is the only thing to eat while on an expedition – this was bottom of Hamish's list, and fresh food and tinned produce formed the bulk of his intake. Of course, the back-up team was essential in supplying much of this. Forty-two food parcels, each containing highly nutritious and calorie-packed provisions, were placed in advance at various strategic points around the Highlands.

Yet on any large-scale expedition, there are occasions when no amount of experience and planning can radically improve the situation. Continual bad weather, battering rain and wind can exaggerate the scale and loneliness of the Scottish hills to the point where despair and hopelessness demoralise the very spirit which took the individual to the hills in the first place. Hamish was at just such a trough on 10 June, when he had only 100 Munros to go. He had left Oban bothy at the east end of Loch Morar, heading for the wilds of Knoydart. As bad weather closed in, he began to get wetter and colder and realised that hypothermia was not far away. He decided to pitch his tent, only to discover that the tent pegs were back at the bothy. The only solution was to grovel about in the icy wetness, collecting rocks to hold the tent. He describes crawling into his sleeping-bag, where it took half an hour and a couple of brews before his shivering stopped.

His main concern was that the bad weather would continue and prevent him from scaling the Knoydart Munros according to plan, thus causing him to fall behind schedule. Worry tends to breed more worry and this was certainly the case on that particular night, the lowest point of the whole trip.

Of course, on any expedition there will be low points and high points. This is what creates the rich tapestry of the total experience, but for that experience to be positive and uplifting the latter must predominate, which they undeniably did on Hamish's walk.

Hamish's Mountain Walk, the book describing the remarkable 112-day odyssey, did not appear on the shelves until 1978 and until then Hamish Brown was a regular contributor to both *Climber and Rambler* magazine and the *Glasgow Herald*. The impact of the book was quite phenomenal and it would be no exaggeration to say that its publication was one of the most crucial spurs to potential Munroists. By the end of the Seventies the Munroist count had reached 200 and by the mid-Eighties it had doubled to 400.

Hamish's descriptive writing, like Tom Weir's, has a sharpness and immediacy which almost breathe the freshness and beauty of the mountain scene. It is the kind of book which one can dip into anywhere and catch the narrative within seconds, so it can be read again and again without any loss of sparkle. Like Borthwick's *Always a Little Further* or Murray's *Mountaineering in Scotland*, it will always have its assured place in the annals of Scottish mountaineering literature. Although the book is basically a day-by-day account of the trip, there are countless diversions in the way of recollections, reminiscences, historical snippets, opinions and humorous anecdotes that enrich and enliven the general flow.

As Hamish Brown is such an instrumental and central character in the Munro phenomenon, it is fitting at this point to examine his persona in more detail. Apart from seeing the man on one of his numerous slide lectures, I first met Hamish at his home in the early part of 1994. Overlooking the Firth of Forth, the setting of his house reflects his other passions of canoeing and tall ships, although I did not expect to find this bearded beacon of the outdoors living in a fairly modern bungalow in a small housing estate! However, once inside, my expectations were fulfilled. Shelves and boxes of books lined the hall-way, living-room and study, whilst numerous Moroccan artifacts decorated the walls. Hamish's lifestyle of mountaineering, travelling and writing is perfectly reflected in his interior décor.

As I made myself comfortable in the living-room resemblances to a mountain-bothy interior soon made themselves plain – including the open log stove and assorted draughts. Hamish, clad in a chunky pullover, sandals and woolly socks completed the picture as he emerged from the kitchen with two mugs of coffee.

Our conversation ranged from Munros to Morocco, probably the two greatest interests in his life over the past 30 years or so. For all of this time, Hamish has made regular three-month annual excursions to the Atlas mountains, where he stays with a local family and guides private groups into the mountains. Although his first love is Scotland, he is increasingly dissatisfied with the 'mob mentality' on Scottish hills and regards the Atlas as a relatively unfrequented haven of peace and solitude. His thirst for a 'back-to-basics' mode of life is quenched totally in Morocco and he is often depressed on returning to the petty sham of so-called civilised Britain. His time spent on the Munros has lessened over the last few years and he now heads for the really out-of-the-way, wild places in Scotland, such as remote lesser hills and islands. Having said this, by the time this book is published Hamish will already have a new book in circulation entitled *The Last Hundred*, intended as a companion volume to Muriel Gray's *The First Fifty* (described later in this chapter).

During our chat Hamish disappeared and returned with a massive volume containing a record of his experiences on the Scottish hills over his life-time. When he then informed me that this hefty book was only a summary of his stravaigings my jaw dropped in amazement. His 'office' housed a further 36 bound volumes in detailed diary form – these obviously formed the basis of many of his books. My impression of a man utterly immersed in the great outdoors, Scotland and its mountains was further enhanced when he showed me his complete set of *SMC Journals* dating back to their conception in 1891.

Inevitably, the conversation centred around Munros, particularly his 'long walk' in 1974 and the controversial revision of Munro's Tables in 1981 (which is discussed fully in Appendix 1). Hamish was quick to stress that he was not out to break any records in his continuous Munro traverse. His only aim was to complete all the Munros under his own propulsion – the timescale was irrelevant. Since he was the first person to complete a continuous round of the Munros anyway, there was no existing record to be broken.

At one point I asked him his Munroist number and he replied that he hadn't a clue. This observation reflected a general characteristic of Hamish's make-up – a dislike of numbers and statistics which even extends to guide-books and guide-book information. 'I've nothing personally against guide-books,' he says. 'The sheep follow them but not me.' Even when he was discussing a proposed future traverse of the Atlas mountains, he admitted to having no idea of the distance involved. He abhors the modern-day obsession with records, times and statistics but accepts that there is nothing wrong with people 'doing their own thing' on the mountains as long as they enjoy themselves and do not harm the mountain environment.

Despite Hamish's prolific literary outpourings, he does not possess a typewriter, preferring to send all his handwritten material to a typist. Not surprisingly, he regards computers and word-processors with a disparaging contempt. It was remarked by a visitor to his house that he should computerise his slide collection of literally thousands of transparencies in order to quicken access to a particular slide. 'What's the point?' he asks. 'I can lay my hands on any picture in under a minute' – and to prove his point he did, several times. Nor does television play any role in Hamish's life. He does not possess one, and with the steady stream of drivel being produced it is easy to sympathise with him.

While on the subject of long walks, I had mentioned John Merrill and his British coastal walk some years ago. We both agreed that he didn't seem to have indulged in much walking since then. Hamish then quipped, 'Ah, but he got married, didn't he? That usually puts an end to things!' Also in this vein was the story of a friend of Hamish's whose obsession with mountains and walking caused a rift in his marriage. His wife finally gave him an ultimatum: 'You can have either me or the hills.' He chose the hills. Naturally, Hamish is a bachelor.

The image of Hamish Brown as one of Scotland's most distinguished outdoor ambassadors, thoroughly anchored in the essential fundamentals of life and unburdened by the nine-to-five routine, form-filling bureaucracy and phoney pretensions of modern living is an image which, I suspect, many hill-goers woud like to reflect themselves.

In 1983 a book appeared which was effectively a diary of ascents of the Munros spanning a period of 20 years. *Memorable Munros* (Diadem) by Richard Gilbert suffers somewhat from being written in a rather prosaic, matter-of-fact style, although Gilbert's deep feeling for the mountains shines through in his descriptions. What is communicated effectively in the book is the remarkable passion and zest which drives the Munro-bagger on to completion. Richard Gilbert is probably best known in connection with the three companion volumes, *The Big Walks*, *Classic Walks* and *Wild Walks* (all published by Diadem), which were all compiled by him and Ken Wilson, with Gilbert doing the bulk of the writing.

The Big Walks appeared in 1980 and was to start a trend of large, glossy coffee-table books which encouraged armchair hillwalkers to find their boots and head for the mountains once again. The chief selling-point of this book and the next two in the series is the collection of absolutely stunning photographs by a variety of different photographers. They are not only crystal clear but each captures a mood which symbolises the mountain experience at various seasons of the year. In terms of professionalism and quality, these three books set the high standard which is now the norm for large-format mountaineering books.

Meanwhile, *Hamish's Mountain Walk* inspired other Munro devotees to follow his lead. In 1982 Kathy Murgatroyd became the first (and only) woman to complete a continuous round of the Munros. She reckons that it is 'disgraceful' that no other woman has yet completed a continuous round of the Munros.

Kathy packed in her job as an outdoor-education teacher with Grampian Regional Council in December 1981 to spend a season ski-instructing in the Alps. This gave her the necessary finance and fitness to embark on her marathon Munro quest on 1 May 1982. She finally finished on 11 September, taking 134 days, with the latter part of the trip being replanned due to the stalking season. Like Hamish Brown, Kathy used a bicycle for the road sections but tended to use fixed bases to climb groups of Munros, thus cutting down on the weight she had to carry.

Early on in the trip, she was sitting at a table at one such fixed base, the youth hostel at Crianlarich, when in walked a man with an extremely familiar face – Hamish Brown – though this was the first time the two had ever met. Hamish remembers seeing an attractive, sun-tanned female face in the corner (the tan more as a result of a season skiing in the Alps than of

Kathy Murgatroyd, the first woman to complete a continuous round of the Munros

a Scottish summer!) and making a beeline for that table. She seemed to know he was Hamish Brown even before he had introduced himself but she was determined not to let the cat out of the bag and tell him what she was up to. A second curious quirk of fate occurred almost at the end of her trip when she was on Skye with only the Cuillin Ridge to do to finish the round. Yet *again* by chance she met Hamish Brown, in Glenbrittle, and this time pride got the better of her and she spilled the beans. The two of them must have had plenty to talk about!

On the whole, Kathy was very lucky with the weather, pointing out that she'd completed half the Munros before she got her feet wet – quite a record for a Scottish summer. Like Hamish, she had planned food parcels and back-up in the form of boyfriend Ivan Young and a couple of others.

The elation of finishing was soon followed by tears and it was literally months before she was able to settle back into a 'normal existence' once again. After over four months of stravaiging round the Scottish Highlands, it is not difficult to see why.

When I visited Kathy at her home in Livingston I asked her if she had ever thought of writing a book about her experiences. She replied that she had actually written half a book but time and motivation were lacking and it did not progress any further. Kathy still works as an outdoor instructor (at Oban) and these days is more involved with sailing than walking the hills. She has a few ideas for new ventures, one of them being to sail a yacht to Iceland – good luck to her! After a most engaging two-hour chat, I noticed a poster on her wall with the caption 'I don't know where I'm going but I'm on my way.' This seemed to sum Kathy up totally – only I think she does know where she is going, and it certainly isn't the road of a bland life which far too many people blindly follow.

It is interesting that other continuous-Munro-round attempts were also made in 1982 but none were successful. One of these was by a man called Dave Herdman, whom Kathy actually met halfway up a Munro, where they swapped stories. Dave unfortunately suffered nutritional deficiencies and failed in his quest with only 12 Munros to go.

Then, in 1984, George Keeping completed the third continuous round in 136 days, and without the use of a bicycle. Not content with that, he added a further 29 days to include the English and Welsh 3,000-foot summits, becoming the first person to traverse the British 3,000-footers (minus Ireland) in a single expedition. This has since been repeated including Ireland but to date the continuous 'Grand Slam' challenge of the Munros, Tops and Furth patiently awaits any takers! Also in 1984, Rick Ansell completed the mainland Munros in 100 days without using a bicycle, but his reasons for omitting the island Munros were decidedly enigmatic – he explained 'the ferries would have spoiled the purity of the walk, which is a good excuse for not feeling competent to solo the Skye ridge!' This omission was a great pity, not only destroying the completeness of the walk but also the chance of breaking Hamish's 112-day 'record', which would have been a distinct possibility.

However, later that year an expedition was begun which was to knock 29 days of Hamish's performance and constitute a monumentally greater challenge – a continuous traverse of the Munros in winter conditions. A young 29-year-old accountant called Martin Moran decided his destiny in life was not to sit behind a desk in a stuffy office. In fact, four years earlier he had handed in his notice with the intention of attempting the round during the winter season 1980–81. His plans were cruelly thwarted, however, when he damaged a knee while training just six weeks before the intended departure date. Luckily, he was re-engaged at his office, but the winter Munro dream, was still alive in his mind as he returned to the drudgery of ledger-sheet accounts. Four years later the dream was finally realised.

Martin and Joy Moran, during Martin's epic 83-day traverse of all the Munros in winter

Like Hugh Munro and W.H. Murray, Martin Moran's affinity for the Scottish mountains in winter was boundless, and many other mountaineers of today also extol the virtues of Scotland's wilderness country when in the grip of snow and ice. For it is only then that the mountains' great potential for adventure is maximised to the full. The days are shorter, the weather more unpredictable, the objective dangers more apparent and extremes become the norm. From pleasant ridge-walking on a sharp, ice-bound crest to an ungainly flounder in a snow-choked gully. From a glorious downhill run on Nordic skis to a gruelling uphill battle in the teeth of a gale. All these would be experienced in the great winter Munro challenge. Above all, it is the majestic beauty of Scotland's winter mountains which provide the inspiration to contemplate such a feat. A snow-plumed ridge crest unfurling against the background of an azure sky, with wind-sculptured cornices balanced precariously above vast, snow-bound corries is a sight to quicken the pulse and galvanise the winter mountaineer into performing distinguished deeds.

The timing of Martin Moran's 'distinguished deed' was of the utmost importance – after all, when is 'winter' in the mountains? Most would reply, 'when there is snow on the hills'. But then the first snows of winter can appear in early October and it is common for some mountains to hold snow well into May. On the other hand, the skiers' nightmare of bare hills in January has often come true, particularly over the last few years. In a technical sense, the winter season could be said to last from 21 December to 20 March, and this is the period when true winter ascents can be claimed in the Alps. This was the period finally decided on, and it gave Martin a rather tight winter window of 90 days in order to complete the gargantuan

A triumphant
Martin Moran on
Sgurr Eilde Mor

The traverse of the Creag Meagaidh range north of Loch Laggan was planned for the following day, 26 January. The idea was that the whole party would climb the first Munro of Carn Liath, then split, with the skiers (Martin, Chris and Hamish) completing the other four Munros. However, the best-laid schemes were soon to be dashed, and the following morning Chris discovered that his Nordic skis had been stolen from his car roof-rack. Hamish's dog Storm abruptly disappeared in thick snow cover minutes after going outside, and Hamish, being inseparable from his canine companion, decided that he could only manage a few hours out. So for most of the day Martin enjoyed his own company, albeit in perfect sunny conditions with sparkling snow peaks stretching in every direction. The final twist occurred when Martin reached the road at 6.30 p.m. The lay-by meeting point was deserted, and a cold, shivering climber was eventually picked up by his wife, who had been waiting at an identical lay-by two miles up the road.

Such was the ebb and flow of daily life on this formidable 83-day epic. The full story of the trip is marvellously recounted in Martin Moran's *The Munros in Winter* (David and Charles), published in 1986, and is truly compulsive reading for all lovers of the Scottish mountains. Martin's fundamental recipe for success was his fast, lightweight movement and efficient and morale-boosting back-up. However, he was also extremely fortunate in having chosen one of the most settled winters for a decade, with the incidence of gales and snowfall little over half their averages.

Martin's Munro trip finished on 13 March on Sgurr Eilde Mor in the Mamores. The extremely settled winter was followed by the wettest summer in Scotland this century. This, of course, was of little consequence to Martin, who was now basking in the glory of the fastest Munro round ever – and, more importantly, it had been undertaken completely in winter.

But somewhere in the rain-lashed Highlands of the summer of 1985 a lone figure named Craig Caldwell was attempting the unthinkable. Could there be an even greater challenge than the Munros in winter? Craig had set himself the truly monumental challenge of climbing all the Munros *and* Corbetts in a single self-propelled journey – a total of 498 peaks. Just as Hugh Munro had sparked off the sport of Munro-bagging, Hamish Brown appeared to have done the same with continuous Munro traverses – but Craig's intended feat was far beyond this, though certainly inspired by continual Munro rounds. It is indeed a reflection of Craig's remarkable resilience and determination that to date no repeat Munro/Corbett round has ever been recorded. This is perhaps not surprising, considering that Craig's remarkable odyssey lasted over a year. Few people have the time or inclination to tackle a four-month round of the Munros, let alone a year on Munros and Corbetts.

Craig Caldwell, the first and probably only person to complete a continuous round of all the Munros and Corbetts

Many folk would question the motives of someone embarking on a year-long tramp round the Highlands and Islands, and indeed of a continuous traverse of the Munros. Suffice to say, like Hamish Brown and Martin Moran before him, Craig Caldwell has a passionate love of the Scottish Highlands, which is surely the overriding prerequisite for undertaking such a trip. There are few people who would intentionally endure endless weeks of rain, wind, midges, mist and gut problems without possessing an almost obsessive passion for the land they are walking in. Craig was incredibly unlucky in having chosen the wettest summer since 1897, and out of an active 300 days on the hill only 55 were totally clear.

Like Martin Moran, Craig used his efforts to benefit a charity, and he succeeded in raising an incredible £18,000 for the Erskine Hospital for ex-servicemen. However, oddly enough, the idea for fund-raising did not occur until Craig's walk was underway.

Barely a month before Martin Moran completed his epic winter walk over all the Munros, Craig Caldwell began his 13-month escapade on 16 February 1985 in the Border hills. His idea was to complete the Border and Galloway Corbetts first, then island-hop up from Arran to Jura and Mull, and eventually on to the Outer Hebrides. The Arrochar Alps were also tackled after Arran. The mainland peaks were then tackled in a north-south direction, finishing with the easier hills of Perthshire and the Trossachs and finally Ben Lomond on 27 February 1986. Craig benefited enormously

66

from an excellent support team, including his mother and father and numerous friends.

Climb Every Mountain, the aptly titled book of Craig's walk (published by MacDonald), did not appear until 1990, four years after his completion, the time-lag perhaps being a reflection of the amount of research and preparation. The book invites obvious comparison with *Hamish's Mountain Walk* and though similar in style, particularly its numerous historical snippets, the narrative is stamped with a freshness and individuality unique to the author. Despite the poor weather Craig's sense of humour still enlivens the day-to-day narration of events.

In the autumn of 1985 a book appeared which was destined to become a bestseller, catering for a potential readership already crying out for its publication. *The Munros*, published by the Scottish Mountaineering Club, quickly became the 'Bible' of the Munro-bagger. It was the first of the SMC's new-style, new-format guide-books with colour prints throughout on good-quality paper – yet retailing at the remarkably low price of £10.95. The book was edited by the highly respected Donald Bennet, who together with such names as Hamish Brown and Bill Brooker has contributed to the many sections.

Literally months after the publication of *The Munros*, in the spring of 1986, another colourful Diadem classic was published. *The High Mountains* (of Britain and Ireland) by Irvine Butterfield was also aimed at the Munro-baggers market but extended the repertoire to include the 3,000-foot peaks of England, Wales and Ireland. Unlike *The Munros*, this large volume was certainly not designed to slide into a rucksack, and its considerable weight and bulk placed it in the coffee-table-book category. However, whatever it lacked in compactness was made up for a hundredfold in style, presentation and above all the magnificent selection of full-colour photographs, the cornerstone of Diadem's success with books of this nature. The photos are a mouth-watering collection which are not only of topographical value but also have inspirational and creative appeal.

Irvine Butterfield is very much a traditionalist and he does not go along with many of the recent changes in Munro's Tables. This is reflected in *The High Mountains*, and a few of the hills described are demoted to 'Tops' in the revised Tables or, like Beinn an Lochan, have now become new Corbetts. His total tally is 610 Tops throughout the British Isles, of which 300 are given full mountain status.

The similar subject matter of *The Munros* and *The High Mountains* invites comparisons between the two. Although they both tackle a common problem efficiently, they do so in essentially different ways. *The Munros* is basically a one-route-per-page guide-book with the ascent of one or more Munros described. *The High Mountains* divides the hills of Britain and

Ireland into 30 separate and manageable groups, giving a brief overview of each group before continuing with detailed route descriptions. From the point of view of style, presentation and photography, this book wins hands down. *The Munros*, on the other hand, is the more convenient and compact guide-book.

Whatever the individual merits of these two books, one thing is sure: they both had a powerful effect on the continuing exponential rise in Munro collectors and on hillwalkers generally.

With vastly increased numbers of 'compleat' Munroists, it was inevitable that lesser peaks began to receive more attention, and the Corbetts provided a new challenge for incurable peak-baggers. Their lower height (2,500–2,999 feet) does not necessarily make them any less of a challenge. In fact, the statutory 500 feet of re-ascent on all sides almost excludes the possibility of long ridges of easy Corbetts, such as the South Cluanie Ridge, which contains seven Munros.

Not surprisingly, the potential of Scotland's smaller hills had long been recognised by the Scottish Mountaineering Club and its publication *The Corbetts and Other Scottish Hills* followed in 1990, only five years after *The Munros*. According to Hamish Brown, this companion volume to *The Munros* surfaced largely due to his own pushing of the SMC. In fact *his own* book *Climbing the Corbetts* pre-dated the SMC guide by two years. A detailed discussion of Corbetts and other lists can be found in Chapter 9.

In the summer of 1986 another major hurdle was finally realised in the erratic history of continuous mountain traverses. A young man from Clitheroe in Lancashire by the name of Ashley Cooper became the sixth person in history to complete the Munros in a single expedition. More importantly, he also became the first to continue on and complete the 13 Irish, 15 Welsh and eight English 3,000-foot Tops as well – the Munros and Furth in one journey.

The vital spark for this journey was not ignited by the need to be first, but by the entirely unselfish goal of raising money for a well-known charity. Almost a year before, 24-year-old unemployed graduate Ashley had visited friends in Malawi and had been introduced to some of the staff of LEPRA (the British Leprosy Relief Association). There he was informed that £10 can in most cases cure one of the world's 15 million leprosy victims. Armed with this knowledge, Ashley decided on the spot to put his enforced idleness to some really effective use, and the seeds of the Munros and Furth trip were well and truly sown.

On 17 August 1986 Ashley finally completed his 313-peak, 1,420-mile marathon in an entirely self-supporting bid, having raised over £6,000 for LEPRA. Considering that out of the 107 days he took to cover the Munros part of the trip only 14 had been free of rain or snow, this was a truly monumental effort. At the time, his trip drew relatively little publicity but in retrospect the name of Ashley Cooper must certainly rank alongside the other 'Munro giants' of the Seventies and Eighties.

As the Eighties drew to a close several other continuous Munro rounds were attempted, two of them remarkable, though for different reasons. (See Appendix 3 for a complete list of continuous-round Munroists.) In 1988 Mark Elsegood completed all the Munros in the (then) record time of 66 days, but his story and other fell-running exploits will be discussed in the next chapter.

The following year a young lad called Paul Tattersall from Wigan threw mud in the faces of the purists and sceptics by becoming the first person to traverse the Munros with a mountain bike. The word 'with' is significant here, as in many instances Paul resorted to carrying the bike rather than riding it. Although many of Scotland's hills may be suitable for mountain-biking, a vast proportion are patently unsuitable and the very idea of manhandling a bike along, say, the Cuillin Ridge must surely border on the lunatic fringe. Even the free-thinking man of the Munros himself, Hamish Brown, half-joked that 'anyone who takes a bike up the Cuillin needs a psychiatrist'. Having said that, he is always quick to defend the individual's right to enjoy the hills in his own way without fear of adverse criticism.

Nevertheless, just how *do* you get a bike up the Inaccessible Pinnacle? Paul's solution to this, and indeed the whole Cuillin Ridge, was to dismantle

Paul Tattersall on Carn Mor Dearg with Ben Nevis behind, during his mountain-bike traverse of the Munros

the bike, tying the frame to his rucksack and strapping the wheels on top. With 35 pounds of tubular steel and rubber, together with a heavy sack, Paul spent 17½ gruelling hours traversing Britain's most challenging mountain route, and how much more so with a heap of useless metal strapped to his back!

Paul admitted that the bike was as much a nuisance as it was an advantage, saying, 'I found I was able to ride down a surprising number of mountains, using stalkers' paths, but on a lot of the terrain I simply had to carry it up and carry it down again.'

There are those who will dismiss Paul Tattersall as 'a tube with a screw loose' (excuse the pun), but his epic adventure was only the natural outcome of the expanding mountain-biking phenomenon, and for eccentricity the trip is not a patch on taking a piano up Ben Nevis or pushing a dried pea up Snowdon with the end of your nose! (Yes, that has been done.)

Before Paul embarked on his Munro trip he had had very little experience in Scotland. Graduating from Sheffield University in 1985, he then spent two-and-a-half years travelling around Asia, Australia and New Zealand, where his love for mountain-biking first germinated. A subsequent holiday in Scotland saw him ride up seven mountains in the Southern Highlands and it was then that he learned what Munros are. The idea of doing them all on a bike formed in his mind and continued to blossom during another overseas trip, this time to Sudan, Egypt and Israel.

No sooner had Paul returned than be began to plan the route and look for financial backing, but this was easier said than done. 'It's difficult to find backing for a trip of this nature when you're a nobody,' he said. 'People aren't prepared to back you for something they believe has little chance of success.' Certainly, many pundits were predicting failure right from the start but their scepticism soon turned to astonishment when Paul completed the trip in a remarkable 81 days. All the more remarkable considering that he was a relative novice to Scottish hills and the accompanying dreich weather which soon initiated him into the skills of navigation. Only four days into the trip Paul was struggling along the ridge between Ben More and Stob Binnein near Crianlarich in low cloud and rain. He took nearly three hours to complete what would normally be a 20-minute traverse after straying off the route in the thick mist.

His longest and most memorable day was a 19½-hour epic on the Glen Etive hills when he finally arrived back at his tent at 2 a.m. – only to rise three hours later to begin a ten-hour traverse of the Bridge of Orchy hills. A common problem with Munro day-trippers is sometimes having to force an artificial circular route in order to return to a car. 'The beauty of the bike,' said Paul, 'was that I could come down miles from base and cycle back with ease.'

Despite the poor start (weatherwise), the summer of 1989 turned into the best for over a decade – I remember it well as I had spent July backpacking from the Mull of Kintyre to Cape Wrath in wall-to-wall sunshine. The good weather undoubtedly contributed to Paul's success but such was his resolve and determination that he would probably have succeeded whatever the weather.

The obvious extension to Paul's trip would be to include Furth of Scotland, and this challenge still awaits any intrepid mountain-biker out there.

Before closing this chapter on the post-war revolution in Munro-bagging we turn briefly to a media-related aspect whose impact in the rising tide of Munro-baggers should not be underestimated.

The humorous side of Munro-bagging surfaced in 1991 in the form of *The First Fifty – Munro-bagging Without a Beard* (Mainstream), written by television presenter and newspaper columnist Muriel Gray. As the jacket note says: 'It would be hard to think of someone more extraordinary to guide you through the mighty peaks of Scotland than a self-confessed eight-stone peroxide-blonde girl with spindly shanks and a nose that turns blue if not kept at constant room temperature.'

Muriel Gray's unique and infectious brand of humour grabs the reader on every page, and she has a great gift of getting to the nub of the matter in a few irreverent and irrepressible quips. The book is a timely and refreshingly new angle on a now almost obsessive cult pursuit. Those readers looking for sentimental and idealistic aspects of Munro-bagging will not find them here!

It was while Muriel Gray was working on her book that the idea formed for a television programme about Munro-climbing. Muriel's experience of television and her obvious enthusiasm for the sport made her the natural choice for presenter, and in the spring of 1991 *The Munro Show* made its first appearance on Scottish Television, exactly 100 years after Hugh Munro's original list first appeared.

Of course, the idea of a series of TV programmes concentrating on Scotland's wild country was not new, but this was the first to occupy itself totally with Munros, and was inventive and unconventional into the bargain. Its forerunners included the likes of *Weir's Way, MacGregor's Scotland, Wainwright in Scotland* and the esoteric *Where Eagles Fly* series by Hamish MacInnes. These programmes tend to fall into two main categories. The first revolves around a series of supposedly random encounters with various locals, hillwalkers and other more revered country gentlemen such as estate managers. This was the formula the Weir and MacGregor programmes adopted, although the central theme in *MacGregor's Scotland* was the undertaking of a long-distance walk along a

71

route such as the West Highland Way or the Southern Upland Way. The series of six programmes *Where Eagles Fly* falls neatly into the second category, which relies almost completely on the 'breath-catching' approach of assailing the viewer with an endless barrage of aerial mountain vistas, complete with statutory eagle, and all suitably accompanied by the haunting but ultimately bland tones of Moira Kerr. All these programmes work up to a point but inevitably attract only a select fraction of potential viewers.

The interesting point about *The Munro Show* is that rather than avoid the stereotyped categorisation described above, Muriel Gray managed to extract the finest components of each and inject her own individual combination of flamboyant enthusiasm, impish humour and irreverent banter to create a marvellously refreshing and highly watchable series. The sport of Munro-climbing had finally reached the most chronic couch potatoes, some of whom even forsook their perpetual cathode-ray cavalcade of clichéd claptrap to don cagoules and crampons, and discover the true delights of the Scottish mountains from Cairngorm to Conival.

The structure of the programme was simple. Two distinct walks over one or more Munros were described, separated by a short flashy feature on some specific hill-related issue. However, it was the ensemble of disparate features clothing this basic framework which helped give the programme its vital spark of originality. The programme opened with a multi-cultural selection of colourfully booted dancers against the background of an almost subliminal montage of mountain images, complete with a 'get up and go' rap soundtrack. Later in the programme the viewer was presented with the suitably contrasting image of the famous Gaelic bard Sorley MacLean seated in a traditional Scottish schoolroom. With scholarly precision he instructed the viewer in the semantic subtleties of the mountain's name, which was chalked on the blackboard behind him.

Muriel Gray resembles a female version of Oor Wullie with her blonde spiky hair and lithe frame. She appears to leap and dart up mountains dressed in her colourful fleecy jackets, all the while spouting forth her canny observations without becoming in the least bit breathless. Yet she never allows herself to become ridiculous, and when she encounters situations which she found nerve-racking or worrying this fear was conveyed to the viewer with honesty – and humour. For instance, she had no hesitation in describing Aonach Eagach, mainland Britain's narrowest ridge, as a 'brown-underpants job'.

The last programme of the first series broke away from the standard format and was devoted entirely to the climbing of Scotland's hardest Munro, the Inaccessible Pinnacle. Here again, Muriel communicated her trepidation to the viewer and she quite willingly put herself in the safe hands and harness of her bearded male benefactor. Critical comments were made after the first series complaining that Muriel never ventured further east than Creag Megaidh, concentrating only on the narrow ridges and craggier summits of the west. This imbalance was soon rectified in the second series when the Cairngorms and Deeside featured more heavily – even the non-Munro of Suilven had an airing.

There is no doubt that *The Munro Show*, with its novel approach, attracted a whole new cross-section of the public to the delights of the Scottish hills. The aforementioned couch potatoes who were previously only dimly aware of such things as Munros were now 'fledgling' Munroists cutting their teeth on easily accessible peaks like Ben Lomond and Ben Narnain. After all, if a spindly blonde like Muriel Gray could climb Munros then anyone could! In effect, *The Munro Show* brought what was seen as a somewhat macho, pretentious, male-dominated pastime, down to a common level, out of the pub and into the living-room. Yes, women were actually climbing Munros too, and many without the moral or physical support of a bearded male companion!

Yet despite all this, it is known that out of 1,274 Munroists recorded up to August 1994, only 175 of them are women. In other words, less than 14% of Munroists are female. Munro-bagging is therefore still effectively a male pursuit.

In this chapter an attempt has been made to draw together the many and varied influences which have contributed towards the phenomenal rise in the sport of Munro-bagging since the Second World War. Increased leisure time, growing numbers of outdoor books and periodicals and even TV programmes have all made an impact. The mid-Seventies onwards saw the most significant surge in numbers, and the fascination of continuous Munro rounds sparked off by Hamish Brown's 112-day trip in 1974 was certainly instrumental in fuelling the Munro phenomenon.

One final facet of the Munro-bagging boom has not been mentioned at all. However, its development has been deemed so crucial to the present-day record-breaking Munro feats that it warrants a complete chapter to itself. Without it, today's continuous Munro-traverse record would still be Martin Moran's 83 days – it is now 51 days. The fell-running phenomenon is the subject of the next chapter.

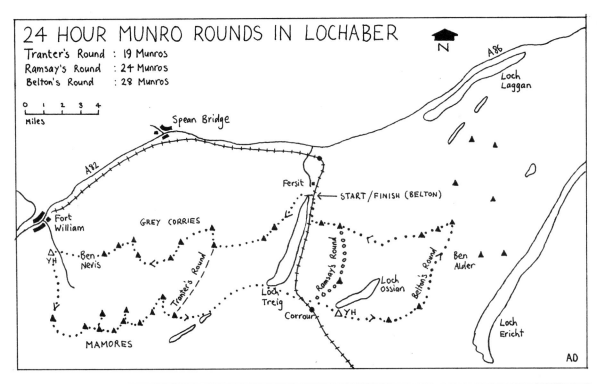

24 HOUR MUNRO ROUNDS IN LOCHABER

Tranter's Round : 19 Munros
Ramsay's Round : 24 Munros
Belton's Round : 28 Munros

Loch Laggan
A86
Spean Bridge
A82
Fersit
START/FINISH (BELTON)
Fort William
GREY CORRIES
Ben Nevis
YH
Ramsay's Round
Tranter's Round
Loch Treig
Corrour
Loch Ossian
Belton's Round
Ben Alder
YH
MAMORES
Loch Ericht
AD

Typical fell-running terrain: Ben Nevis from the Mamore Ridge

CHAPTER 5

The Fell-Running Phenomenon

We were moving fast today. After five hours we were on our way up the final mountain: Beinn Alligin. The heavy early morning cloud was now thinning. We ascended Alligin on a steepening slope of grass and rock. At last, for the first time since An Teallach, mountains were coming into view. The sun was strong and the sky a perfect blue on our arrival at the summit cairn. There wasn't a hint of haze or cloud in the sky. The Cuillins of Skye, Ben Nevis and perhaps a hundred other Munros speckled the skyline. Martin recited their names as Paul and I stood looking in awe in all directions. An Teallach looked distant and my first mountain, Ben Hope, was out of sight. The clearing of the clouds had been like an awakening; a realisation that now, 12 days into the journey, I had travelled beyond the horizon.

Hugh Symonds, *Running High*

The sport of fell-running is strangely unique in that it is almost only practised in the United Kingdom, and by a relatively small band of enthusiasts. Indeed, the sport of hillwalking is very much a British pursuit, and in the Alps or the American Rockies the nearest label would be something like mountain-walking, backpacking or plain hiking. It could be argued that these are all just different names for the same activity – hillwalking. Yet the majority of mountain-walkers, backpackers and hikers travel *through* mountainous country and leave the actual climbing of the peaks to the mountaineers and rock-climbers. Perhaps the term 'peak-bagger' would be more appropriate to the bulk of Britain's hillwalkers, as in effect this is what they are indulging in.

The crucial point here is that the general topography of Britain's hill country is perfectly suited to the types of activity in which hillwalkers and fell-runners participate. The vast majority of hills have easy walking routes to their summits, they are to a large extent treeless and their relatively lower altitude results in the absence of permanent snow cover. In the Himalaya there are trekkers, in the Alps there are mountain-walkers and in America there are hikers, but the good old British hillwalker is a distinctive breed that has evolved in close harmony with the type of terrain unique in this country.

So what of fell-running? This can be seen as a natural extension from hillwalking into faster mountain travel. The discerning reader may well ask: why fell-running and not hill-running? The simple answer would appear to be that the sport originated in the north of England and in particular the Lake District where many hills are commonly known as fells – thus fell-walking is also a popular pastime.

Many a hillwalker on leaving the summit of perhaps the last Munro of the day will saunter with carefree exhilaration down a broad, easy ridge with an extra inch in their step. Some throw caution to the wind and go that bit further – they begin to run. A few of this last group find that the invigorating elation produced by this simple increase in locomotion is almost akin to skiing, and a few of these take up fell-running.

The added exhilaration of fast downhill running cannot be denied but it is the uphill sections that really sort out the men from the boys. The level of stamina required for long fell runs is quite phenomenal and no amount of hillwalking can adequately prepare the potential fell-runner – he or she will also need a solid basis of running on the flat to provide the necessary foundation for moving into this élite domain.

As with other outdoor activities, the Thirties saw a big upsurge in fell-running. Indeed, the sport as it is known today originated then. The set piece of long-distance fell-running was the Bob Graham Round in the Lake District, a traverse of 42 peaks involving 27,000 feet of ascent and covering a distance of 60 miles. The route began in Keswick, crossed Skiddaw, Blencathra, Helvellyn, the Langdales, Scafell, the Gables and Honister before returning to Keswick by the Newland Fells. In 1932 Bob Graham completed this circuit within 24 hours, and an unbelievable 28 years passed before the round was repeated. Today the record stands at a remarkable 13 hours 53 minutes by Billy Bland in 1982.

However, during the Sixties and Seventies the celebrated Joss Naylor together with Alan Heaton extended Bob Graham's original round, and in June 1975 Joss set a record of 72 peaks within 14 hours, which was to survive for 13 years. Then on 18 June 1988 a relative newcomer to the scene, Mark McDermott, completed an astounding round of 76 peaks, 87 miles and 39,000 feet of ascent within 23 hours 26 minutes. On analysis, such a feat is mind-boggling – the thought of keeping up an average of three peaks and over 1,500 feet of ascent every hour for 24 hours is not one which can be readily accepted without awe and admiration.

Not surprisingly, the allure of 24-hour fell-running rounds spread to Wales and Scotland. Paddy Buckley's Round in Wales traversed 47 peaks with 27,700 feet of ascent in a distance of 61 miles, but the first sub-24-hour round did not fall to Paddy but to Martin Stone in 1985. It is to Scotland that we now turn our attention and specifically to 24-hour Munro rounds.

In 1964 Philip Tranter, son of the highly acclaimed historical novelist Nigel Tranter, became the first person to complete two rounds of the Munros. But in the same year he also had another claim to fame. Starting in Glen Nevis, he traversed all 11 Munros of the twisting Mamores Ridge before crossing Glen Nevis and embarking on another long traverse of the Grey Corries Ridge, finishing with the four 4,000-footers of Aonach Beag, Aonach Mor, Carn Mor Dearg and Ben Nevis – a total of 19 Munros, 40 miles and 20,600 feet of ascent, and, at 23 hours, within the statutory one-day time.

Comparing 'Tranter's Round' with the greater mileage and footage of Bob Graham's Round, it was obvious that Tranter's time of 23 hours would soon be beaten. Today's record stands at 12 hours 50 minutes by Mark McDermott in May 1990. Sadly, Philip Tranter was killed in a car accident in 1966 while returning from a climbing trip to Turkey.

It ought to be noted that Philip Tranter was essentially a hillwalker and not a fell-runner, and his 23-hour round was undertaken as a long walk with all the usual gear required, such as boots and rucksack. The inclusion of five more Munros further east in the Loch Treig area was an idea conceived by Charlie Ramsay, bringing the total to 24 Munros. It is a route which requires pure fell-running tactics to complete. Charlie Ramsay's Ròund became the definitive 24-hour challenge in Scotland – 24 Munros in 24 hours had a definite ring about it.

Prior to Charlie's attempt in 1978, he spent six months in rigorous training, running and walking 1,600 miles and climbing 270,000 feet. Every inch of the proposed route was checked and memorised and four checkpoints were chosen and subsequently manned by members of the Lochaber Mountain Rescue team.

Midday of 8 July 1978 saw Charlie Ramsay, Bobby Shields and three pacers leave the Glen Nevis Youth Hostel to begin the initial traverse of the Mamores, which they accomplished in seven-and-a-half hours, despite thick mist and drizzle threatening to put a damper on the whole trip. The relatively easier option of Tranter's route was now forsaken and an incredibly rough and tiring 11-mile, cross-country eastwards extension was made to reach Beinn na Lap, a remote Munro above Loch Ossian. By this time darkness had fallen and Ramsay recalls becoming depressed and cold, having to put on all his clothing.

The route continued north over the Munros of Chno Dearg and Stob Coire Sgriodain before dropping down to a checkpoint at Loch Treig dam. At this juncture Shields was forced to give up with a sore knee and Ramsay continued on with a new pacer. A long northerly ridge took them to the summit of Stob a'Choire Mheadhoin and Stob Coire Easain, where they began to head west again to Stob Ban, and Tranter's route once again. Here dawn broke to reveal curtains of mist enveloping the Mamores which they had traversed 12 hours before.

They now had eight hours to complete the Grey Corries Ridge, the Aonachs and Ben Nevis – just seven more Munros. However, as at the beginning of the trip, thick mist again came down and Charlie was to lose his route twice, once on the Grey Corries and also, more crucially, coming off Aonach Beag. Here he descended west instead of north to Aonach Mor, and was 1,000 feet down the hill before painfully realising that he had made a heart-rending error, ultimately costing him 40 minutes of valuable time.

It was almost 10 a.m. when he reached Aonach Mor and he had a little over two hours to drag his exhausted body up and over Ben Nevis. The dream was balanced on the knife-edge of failure and success. A sudden clearance of mist from the Ben provided the vital spark of inspiration required, and it was 11.25 a.m. when he stood at the summit of Ben Nevis. The final hurtling descent to the glen 4,000 feet below was more like a controlled fall than run and during the descent he left all his pacers far behind. He reached Glen Nevis Youth Hostel with just two minutes to spare at 11.58 a.m., and Ramsay's Round became a 24-hour reality.

Within the next few years two attempts were made but both of these failed to meet the 24-hour deadline. In 1980 Eddie Campbell recorded a time of 24 hours 40 minutes. A similar time was clocked by Pete Simpson in 1981, his solo effort in wind and rain having been cruelly thwarted within the last hour. He had attempted the route in the opposite direction to Ramsay's original round and was left with 55 minutes to descend to Glen Nevis from his last summit of Mullach nan Coirean. As is often the case in long mountain jaunts, concentration lapsed on the descent and he became hopelessly entangled in thick forestry plantations. A scratched and totally dispirited Pete Simpson finally emerged from his Sitka-spruce shackles to arrive at the youth hostel 40 minutes out of time.

The concentration of Munros in the area west of Fort William and the presence of Ben Nevis were the main reasons why Ramsay's Round became the classic Scottish 24-hour circuit. Various murmurings, especially by Jon Broxap, a youth-hostel warden from Keswick, were made about the possible extension of Ramsay's Round to include the two Munros of Sgor Gaibhre and Carn Dearg lying to the south of Loch Ossian. This would add an extra ten miles and 3,000 feet of ascent and bring the total to 70 miles, 31,000 feet of ascent and 26 Munros. The fact that Ramsay's original round had only been completed two minutes inside the 24-hour deadline made this new round look utterly impossible within the same time limit.

Yet in 1987 Broxap's challenge was taken up by a seasoned long-distance runner by the name of Martin Stone (already mentioned), a 28-year-old computer analyst. Stone is a purist among fell-runners, eschewing support groups or pacers, and he carried all his gear and food in a small rucksack and various zipped pockets around his body.

The morning of 25 June saw him set off up the tourist path on Ben Nevis equipped with five pounds of food and four pounds of gear, including torches and an exposure bag. Perfect weather accompanied him all day, and by the evening he had left Ramsay's route to include the two extra Munros south of Loch Ossian. Darkness never fell totally and the pale, almost phosphorescent glow of the Northern Lights produced enough light to allow him to dispense with the torch, despite there being no moon.

On the long night section back west to the Mamores and on the push up to Sgurr Eilde Mor, Martin had severe problems with drowsiness as his body cried out for sleep, and on three occasions he actually nodded off. As dawn broke on the summit, his biological clock switched on and gave him the vital impetus to traverse the full Mamore Ridge in an incredible six hours. The hostel was reached 36 minutes within the magic 24-hour limit and a new record of 26 Munros in a day had been established.

Martin Stone in the Mamores, checking the route he would subsequently use to add two more Munros to Charlie Ramsay's 24

The original Ramsay's Round of 24 Munros has now been completed by about ten runners and the record stands at 18 hours 23 minutes, set by Adrian Belton on 2 August 1989.

With more and more Munros being completed in a 24-hour period a burning question was beginning to loom. How many Munros could be climbed in a day? A few thought that Martin Stone's record of 26 had to be the limit, while others began to look further afield to the likes of the Shiel-Affric hills, where a sufficient concentration of Munros made a similar challenge seem possible. As far back as 1977, Blyth Wright, an instructor at Glenmore Lodge, had completed a circuit of the Glen Shiel hills in 23 hours, including the well-known South Cluanie Ridge and Five Sisters Ridge – a total of 17 Munros. As this was essentially a walk, it appeared that his circuit could be readily extended to include more Munros, with the obvious adoption of fell-running tactics.

Jon Broxap, who had initiated the extension to Ramsay's Round, was the first person to adopt the challenge and he devised a massive northwards extension to Wright's circuit including some of the Glen Affric hills as well. Without going south to the Quoich hills, there are a total of 30 Munros in the Shiel-Affric area. Broxap planned to do 28 of these within 24 hours.

In 1988 Broxap had decided to emigrate to Australia and before going he wished to perform a suitably Scottish parting enterprise that would live on in his memory and provide inspiration for others. The Shiel-Affric

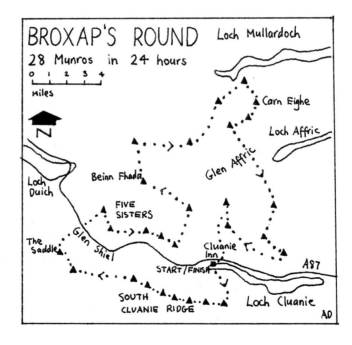

28-Munros-in-a-day-man Jon Broxap enjoys Weetabix and fruit on his first rest stop

round of 28 Munros in a day was the perfect event, and at 10 a.m. on 25 June Broxap left the Cluanie Inn to begin his amazing farewell odyssey. His flight to Australia was booked for the following day, so no second chance was available – it was now or never.

His initial pace was resolutely fast and he knocked off the nine Munros of the South Cluanie Ridge (including the Saddle) in around four hours. After dropping to the road in Glen Shiel, he had his first ten-minute break with an easily digestible mix of fruit and Weetabix. The day was warm and sunny and the necessary liquid intake of one-and-a-half pints per hour made extraordinary demands on Broxap's helpers.

A relentless slog took him on to the North Shiel Ridge and after nine hours from Cluanie Inn he was standing on Ciste Dubh with 15 Munros under his belt. At this physical and psychological halfway stage, success seemed certain, but the long night section over the Affric tops was still to come and it was too early to make optimistic forecasts. Indeed, as one of the pacers was descending from Sgurr nan Ceathreamhnan in the dark he tripped and fell headlong – luckily landing on grass. The incident was a warning signal to slow down and increase concentration.

Dawn began to break as Jon once again crossed Glen Affric to begin the final five Munros of the Loch Cluanie horseshoe with six hours left. Mullach Fraoch Choire, the 28th Munro, was reached in good time before the final dash to the Cluanie Inn, reached after a total of 23 hours and 20 minutes. Jon Broxap had climbed a record 28 Munros over a distance of 78

An exhausted Jon Broxap (centre), accompanied by two pacers (Pete Barron and Mark Rigby) at the finish of his 28-Munros-in-a-day marathon. This record remains unbeaten

Adrian Belton on the Grey Corries Ridge during his 24-hour traverse of 28 Munros

miles and 33,000 feet of ascent in a single day – not a bad parting shot before beginning his new life in Australia. (Jon has since returned to live in Britain after failing to settle down in Australia.)

Today, the record of 28 Munros in a day remains just that, despite several attempts to break it. Adrian Belton, who holds the Ramsay's Round record, attempted to add a further four Munros to Martin Stone's extended Ramsay's Round of 26 Munros, thus increasing it to 30 Munros. Belton made two attempts on this mark 3 version of Ramsay's circuit in 1990 but both were thwarted by bad weather. Then in June 1991 Adrian gave it a third shot, successfully duping his usual willing band of pacers into accompanying him yet again on the basis that 'If I succeeded this time, I really would retire from this head-banging game.' Only a few days before the attempt he was laid up in Fort William Hospital after gashing his elbow during the descent of Beinn Bheoil. He had been carrying out a reconnaissance of the eastern extension of Ramsay's Round to see if 32 Munros in 24 hours was a serious possibility!

At 9 a.m. on the morning of Saturday 1 June Adrian Belton, along with pacer Mark Rigby, set off from Fersit Dam in glorious sunshine and blue skies, electing to carry extra water bottles rather than the usual kit. However, on Stob Coire Claurigh, the third Munro of the day, Mark admitted to having left the extra water behind and no more replenishment was available until Aonach Beag. Further problems were presented by Adrian's arm, which had now swollen badly from the elbow to his knuckles.

Various other pacers and helpers appeared in the ensuing miles, plying Adrian with water, sunhat, suncream, food and general words of encouragement. By the time he reached the Mamore ridge Adrian was half an hour ahead of schedule and at Sgurr Eilde Mor 21 Munros had been completed in little over 13 hours.

At this point, however, just prior to the long night section, Adrian's luck began to change. Precious time was wasted trying to locate the next pacer and Adrian slipped down a waterfall, banging his already injured elbow in the process. The long, dark miles to Loch Ossian Youth Hostel took longer than expected and by the hostel they were almost half an hour behind schedule. To add insult to injury, a wind was already whipping up and mist was descending on the tops. The weather forecast of a cold front coming in seemed to be alarmingly real. Adrian admitted at this stage that he was falling asleep on his feet and lacking willpower – 'If I had been on my own, I would have given up there and then; it was the thought of my long-suffering pacers that inspired me to keep going for their sake. They would never forgive me if I gave up again.' This remark of Adrian's is a bold reflection of just how much the band of pacers make or break such a fell-running attempt; their morale-boosting and physical back-up were obviously absolutely essential to Adrian's eventual success.

Beyond the two Munros south of Loch Ossian the weather deteriorated abysmally and by this time Adrian realised that the far-eastern Munro of Carn Dearg (above Culra Bothy) would have to be abandoned. Mark Rigby, who had already gone out to Carn Dearg, luckily saw Adrian and the other pacers' lights as they crossed the stream below, and he raced back as Adrian battled up Geal Charn in driving snow and bitterly cold winds – in June.

The remaining few Munros were characterised by a 'head-down-and-grit-the-teeth' approach in a near-white-out with the pacers 'doing the most unbelievable job of navigation in what seemed to me to be impossible conditions'. Adrian and his entourage reached Fersit dam just three minutes inside the 24-hour deadline, having climbed 28 Munros and covered 75 miles with 34,000 feet of ascent. In Adrian's own words, 'We were lucky to complete the round with just three minutes to spare, but desperately unlucky to be plagued with such bad weather for the final seven hours. Perhaps I can count this as a simultaneous summer and winter attempt!'

It is almost certain that if the good weather had held, Adrian would have included the eastern Carn Dearg and set a new record of 29 Munros in a day. Beinn na Lap to the north of Loch Ossian would give the total 30, and it is not inconceivable that Ben Alder and its neighbour Beinn Bheoil could also be included – it was on this latter Munro that Adrian injured his arm while reccying the area. It should be noted that Jon Broxap still holds the 28-Munros-in-a-day record, his time being 37 minutes faster than Adrian's.

The natural extension to Broxap's Round would be the two Munros of Tom a' Choinich and Toll Creagach, both lying on the ridge east of Carn Eige though involving an extra 11 miles (including the return). The 30-Munro barrier will be a difficult one to break but with the young, eager, super-fit fell-runners around today it shouldn't be long before this magic figure is reached. Beyond that, it is not so much a matter of fitness as a lack of any 'natural' extension, and the only certainty is that there are sure to be some surprises in the future, as there certainly have been in the past.

Before a brief discussion of other 24-hour challenges, one notable achievement should be mentioned. In July 1990, Mike Hartley completed Ramsay's Round, Bob Graham's Round and Paddy Buckley's Round (a total of 180 miles and 83,000 feet of climbing) in a single outing in the incredible time of 3 days 14 hours 20 minutes. This time includes the two four-hour car journeys between the rounds, during which he snatched some well-earned sleep – a quite astounding feat. Mike Hartley incidentally holds the Pennine Way record of 2 days 17 hours 20 minutes.

In 1954 the Rucksack Club established a long-distance walk connecting all eight 4,000-foot peaks in Scotland. The route begins (or ends) at Glen Nevis Youth Hostel, traverses Ben Nevis and the three other 4,000-foot Lochaber Munros, before an overland trek from Glen Nevis to Glen Feshie and the ascent of the remaining four Cairngorm 4,000-foot Munros, finishing at Glenmore Youth Hostel. The route covers 85 miles and involves some 17,000 feet of ascent.

The one-day barrier for this route was not broken until 1980, when Chris Dodd completed it in 23 hours 14 minutes. Today's record is held by the highly acclaimed Martin Stone in a solo, unsupported attempt on 4 July 1986, in a time of 21 hours 39 minutes.

Literally dozens of runs have been recorded and classified on the major Munro groups: the Arrochar Alps, Glencoe, the Mamores and the Torridon hills to name but a few. One of these groups stands out as being unique, because along with competence in fell-running it also demands climbing tactics. That group is the Black Cuillin Ridge of Skye.

It will be remembered from Chapter 3 that Shadbolt and McLaren became the first climbers to traverse the ridge from end to end in a day. The year was 1911 and their time 12 hours 20 minutes peak to peak. In 1914 Howard Somervell made the first solo traverse in 10½ hours, which set the scene for other soloists such as Bicknell, who in 1932 recorded a time of 8 hours, and D. Stewart, who held the record for many years with a time of 6 hours 45 minutes. Then in 1966 the notable fell-runner Eric Beard, affectionately known as 'Beardie', knocked the time down to an incredible 4 hours 9 minutes, a record which remained unbroken for 18 years. However, he was known to have omitted the Inaccessible Pinnacle.

Andy Hyslop decided to break Eric Beard's 18-year hold on the ridge record, and in 1984 he knocked about five minutes off Beardie's time, as well as taking in all the Munro summits and the four main climbing sections of the Thearlaich-Dubh Gap, King's Chimney on Sgurr Mhic Choinnich, the In. Pin. and the Bhasteir Tooth. Two support points were used and all the climbing sections were soloed without a rope. It goes without saying that Andy had a thorough knowledge of the route beforehand.

Del Davies and Paul Stott then shaved 15 minutes off Andy's record to give a new time of 3 hours 49 minutes, but on 2 June 1990 'Munros in Winter' man Martin Moran cut this by a similar margin to an astounding 3 hours 33 minutes. Finally, in the summer of 1994, Andy Hyslop reclaimed the record by the narrowest of margins, knocking just one minute off Martin Moran's time.

Towards the end of the Eighties numerous fell-runners began seriously contemplating the idea of a continuous run over all the Munros, which would almost certainly crack the 83-day record of Martin Moran's

Hugh Symonds near the summit of Ben Macdui during his remarkble 97-day run over the Munros and Furth (Photo: Matt Dickinson)

winter traverse in 1984–85. Though the idea looked feasible on paper, few runners had the determination and time to push the concept further than a pub conversation. There was not only the couple of months or so involved in the actual run to consider, but also the whole behind-the-scenes organisation of pacers, support groups and other helpers, some or all of which would inevitably be required for such a marathon undertaking.

The first person to take up the challenge was notable fell-runner Mark Elsegood, who used the same tactics as Martin Moran, having a car to drive between the various groups of Munros. He gave himself a fairly generous 75-day schedule which he knew could be comfortably beaten, and in the early summer of 1988 Mark entered the record books with a 66-day round of the Munros.

However, the purists of the fell-running fraternity would not have been satisfied with Mark's run as a car had been used for the road sections. In the spring of the same year another fell-runner by the name of Hugh Symonds, a maths teacher at Sedbergh school in Yorkshire, was on holiday in Scotland with his family. Hugh was no stranger to fell-running and highly respected for his triple wins of the Three Peaks race in Yorkshire, the Ben Nevis race (in 1 hour 27 minutes) and the international 10,000 feet Vignemale in the Pyrenees.

While on holiday, Hugh improved his knowledge of the Scottish hills, of which he had previously had little experience, and in particular running routes. By this time the idea of a continuous run round all the Munros was firmly entrenched in his mind, but how could he fit the schedule into his school summer holiday of 'only' eight weeks? Luckily, Hugh had a far-sighted headmaster who recognised the benefits to teachers and pupils of allowing the staff to take one term's sabbatical every seven years, providing they could come up with a worthwhile venture. When Hugh decided to extend the run to include the mountains of England and Wales and at the same time raise money for Intermediate Technology the whole concept assumed a much grander scale. Hugh received permission from his headmaster with no problem at all – but the pressure to succeed was now intense. To cap it all, he changed his original direction of the run from south-north to north-south, thus finishing on Snowdon in Wales and giving him the option of continuing on to the peaks of Ireland.

Unlike Mark Elsegood, Hugh adhered strictly to a rule of self-propulsion. Although he returned to a mobile home in the evenings, shared with his wife Pauline and three children, this was never used to transport Hugh, but only as a nightly base. The usual ferry crossing to Skye from Kyle to Kyleakin was shunned in favour of a boat crossing of the Sound of Sleat from Glenelg to Kylerhea, the shortest sea route to Skye.

The day before the crossing, Hugh had made an exhausting 23-mile run over the nine Munros on the South Cluanie skyline, climbing 9,000 feet and accompanied by abysmal weather. After leaving the Saddle, the last Munro of the day, he dropped down to Glen More to rendezvous with the van and its welcome home comforts. However, his plan for a pleasant, restful evening followed by a lie-in and short six-mile downhill sprint to Glenelg to row across to Skye at noon the next day, was rudely shattered. A telephone call had revealed that slack tide, the only safe time to row the 500 metres to Kylearhea, would be at 6.45 the next morning. There was no alternative but to run the six miles that evening, thus bringing Hugh's total mileage that day to 29, with the last six done in almost total darkness.

Mull's awkward Munro, Ben More, required a more calculated approach and the idea of rowing the far greater distance was not an option that Hugh readily contemplated. Luckily, he managed to secure the expert services of charter skipper Fearghas McKay, and Hugh helped to steer and sail a 31-foot yacht across the 25-mile Sound of Mull, taking six hours. Thus the self-propulsion philosophy was essentially realised, and Hugh Symonds became the first person to complete a *purely* self-propelled continuous round of the Munros taking just under 67 days. Although only marginally outside Mark Elsegood's time, remember that Mark used motorised transport, including ferries – which makes Hugh's time all the more incredible.

On 24 June 1990, amid the inevitable flourish of publicity, Hugh topped the last Munro of Ben Lomond to end his record-breaking flurry in the wilderness of Scotland. Now all roads led south, and the next day he began his 140-mile stint from Scotland to Skiddaw in England's Lake District. Another adventure was just beginning.

Ironically, after 67 days running in the wild and rugged grandeur of the Scottish Highlands, Hugh discovered that the abrupt assault of Glasgow's traffic and crowds gave him the most anxious and tense time of the entire trip. Road-running is also, curiously enough, harder on the hamstrings than the more varied movement encountered in mountain terrain, and in some ways the long road section to the Lake District proved to be physically and mentally the most draining phase of the venture.

Hugh found a brief respite from the drudgery of roads in the four 3,000-footers of the Lakes before becoming enmeshed in the industrial heartland of north-west England. However, the final 15 Welsh mountains provided the necessary boost, and on 11 July he reached the top of Snowdon, the 296th summit since leaving Ben Hope. Hugh had succeeded in accomplishing a continuous self-propelled traverse of all the 3,000-foot mountains in Scotland, England and Wales in 83 days – the same time Martin Moran had taken for his winter traverse of the Munros.

As if this wasn't enough, Hugh now intended to cross over to southern Ireland and finish with its seven 3,000-footers. Unfortunately, the self-propulsion concept had to be abandoned on the sea crossing to Ireland, and even securing a place on the ferry proved no easy matter. However, on 25 July Hugh stood proudly on the romantic summit of the most westerly 3,000-foot mountain in the British Isles, Brandon Mountain, after leaving the most northerly summit 97 days before. Within this time he had run a distance of 2,048 miles and climbed 500,000 feet over 303 separate mountains. The ultimate accolade came from legendary northern fell-runner Joss Naylor when he commended Hugh's determination and discipline by describing the run as 'perhaps the greatest athletic achievement ever'. Further testimony to the enormity of the feat was given when a subsequent TV programme was shown about the run.

In the months following, the physical discipline of running was replaced by the mental discipline of writing, and in the autumn of 1991 *Running High* (Lochar) made its appearance on the bookshelves. The book is an engrossing and highly readable account, in diary form, of the day-to-day events, hopes and fears of a man with a remarkable resolution and dogged dedication to reach a personal goal. An interesting and appealing feature of the book is the inclusion of Pauline's diaries, which give refreshing views of the female perspective in what could be considered as rather a male-dominated, macho enterprise. Finally, the innocent, laconic remarks in the children's diaries, besides being highly humorous, contain acute observations which add enormously to the book's overall charm.

Like other athletic feats, fell-running records are inevitably transient and only serve to provide the bait for the next aspiring record-breaker. Despite this, the continuous run of all the British and Irish 3,000-foot peaks in under 100 days is likely to remain unrepeated for quite some time. However, the Scottish part of the challenge – the Munros – was inexorably destined to furnish the fell-runner with fresh challenges and the 67-day round remained a record for only two years.

Hugh's statistics show that his average time out per day was around eight hours; or, put another way, 16 hours of every day was spent resting, eating or sleeping. It was clear to most fell-runners that the average eight hours per day running time could be extended to perhaps 12 hours or beyond, and such an extension seemed necessary if any significant reduction on 67 days was to materialise.

Suitably inspired by the likes of Hugh Symonds and Martin Moran, two determined young men by the names of Andrew Johnstone and Rory Gibson decided to meet the challenge in the summer of 1992. Both are 'old boys' of Glenalmond College in Perthshire, an independent school which boasts a highly popular hillwalking and climbing club, some of the present pupils having climbed over 100 Munros. It is ironic that neither Andrew nor Rory participated in this activity at school, Rory preferring to ski and Andrew being heavily involved with cricket and, perhaps inevitably, running.

Andrew did not begin climbing Munros until he was about 23 and had a tally of around 80 before he and Rory embarked on their record-breaking round. Both men immersed themselves in a disciplined and sustained training period, much of this time being spent in the Himalaya, where Rory reached a highly respectable fifth place in the famous Everest Marathon from base camp to the Sherpa capital of Namche Bazaar. There is a nice touch of irony here in that whereas many climbers use Scotland as a training ground for the Himalaya, here were two fell-runners doing the exact opposite. Both men also possessed a solid experience of running, with Andrew having participated in numerous triathlon events.

Rory Gibson and
Andrew Johnstone
running and cycling
during their record
51-day traverse of
all the Munros

Like Munro mentor Hamish Brown 18 years before them, Andrew and Rory saved a ferry trip and started their journey with Ben More on Mull – but his time of 112 days was to be more than halved by these two resolute 32-year-olds. For the first month they were blessed with extraordinarily settled and warm weather, which no doubt contributed to the success of the venture. The self-propulsion ethic was strictly adhered to (apart from the island ferries), with push-bikes being used on the road sections. Theirs was also the first continuous round of the Munros where swimming was used to gain access to a peak – Ben Lomond was reached by swimming half a mile across Loch Lomond, rather than the long cycle trip round the southern end of the loch.

Although they averaged 12-hour days, many were obviously much longer than this and on day 15 of the trip they did not finish until 3 a.m. On that particular day they had climbed three fairly awkward Munros to the west of Glen Etive before arriving at the roadside at 6 p.m. to then cycle up the road to Ballachulish and climb the two Munros forming the horseshoe above the village. After only eight hours' rest the pair were off again at 11 a.m. to tackle the Glencoe Munros. It was Andrew's parents who wisely suggested that the following day should be a rest day, the first, and indeed the only one of the entire trip.

As with other Munro marathons, Andrew and Rory were served with an excellent back-up team providing food, rest and moral support along the way. No pacers were used and the two relied on each other to give encouragement when low points were reached. On the Cuillin Ridge they secured the services of Geoff Charleton from Tomintoul, who guided them over the technical difficulties and 11 Munros in a period of two days – the weather at this time was poor, with little or no visibility. With the exception of Rory spraining his ankle on the fifth day and Andrew coming down with dysentery in Knoydart, the trip unfolded smoothly and according to plan, and on 13 July 1992, 51 days after leaving Ben More, they stood triumphantly on the summit of Ben Hope. The TV and press closely followed Andrew and Rory's progress throughout the period of the attempt and a Grampian TV programme of the event was screened in 1993.

Andrew very modestly states that he sees himself and Rory among the last of the amateur athletes to attempt a record round of the Munros and that their time of 51 days will easily be beaten by professional fell-runners with efficient and organised back-up teams. He shamelessly admits that he is over 12 stone and is partial to the odd pint of beer – he certainly deserves it.

Andrew and Rory's average of between five and six Munros per day is certainly a striking statistic but it would appear to be within the realms of plausibility for this to be increased to around seven – this would give a round of about 40 days. Inevitably, the 50-day barrier will be broken within the next few years, with the precedent of 51 days set by Andrew and Rory providing the necessary inducement. Like any other field of human endeavour, it would be foolish to make predictions about the ultimate achievement possible – perhaps the Munros within a single calendar month could be considered to have 'ultimate-challenge' status, giving an average of nine Munros per day. Such a daunting feat would require not only immaculate planning, strategy and execution together with a superfit team, but also a staggering amount of good luck with the weather and other random factors. 'The Munros in a month' has an obvious ring about it and one can easily envisage this being the title of the inevitable book if such an awesome feat was ever accomplished.

The limits of all this in terms of human endurance can be seen in better perspective if we imagine how long a team of runners would take to climb all the Munros using a relay system. This was in fact accomplished by a team of seven fell-runners in June 1990, taking a total time of just 12 days 17 hours and 8 minutes. The team ran day and night with one or more runners running as a single unit at any one time, i.e. there was no overlap, and the only rule was for the baton to complete the journey. It should be noted that vehicles were used on the road sections, and a more purist approach would necessarily take longer. Nevertheless, the phenomenal average of 21 Munros per day is quite astonishing.

Three years later, in June 1993, a second Munro relay was attempted, again with seven runners, with a target of averaging one Munro per hour, giving an overall goal of 11 days 13 hours. However, from the rain-lashed Skye start in the Cuillin to a similar finish on Ben Hope the attempt was plagued by bad weather, especially during the last three days. Although much of the remainder of the time was relatively settled, with one excellent day, cold, drizzly fog was experienced and one night of severe frost. The weather and a serious sprained ankle destroyed the hopes of reaching the target time, but 11 days and 20 hours beat the existing record by almost a full day.

Anyone reading this chapter thus far could be excused for feeling quite out of breath just contemplating the awe-inspiring feats described. They could also be excused for questioning the motivation of people who indulge in such deeds. Critics of fell-running accuse devotees of the sport of turning the hills into a race-track. They also believe that fell-runners are denying themselves the aesthetic perspective and are only indulging in their epic feats as a challenge and to boost their own ego.

Certainly the basis for many of these feats is the challenge they provide, but this is essentially the springboard for all mountaineering excursions, from a simple walk up the tourist path on Ben Lomond to a proposed 40-day round of all the Munros. As for ego-boosting, it should be pointed out that the majority of fell-runners are a pretty unselfish lot who will go out of their way to help their own kind by way of pacing or to help provide a back-up team. It cannot be denied that on completion of, say, Ramsay's Round in the fastest time or the quickest round of the Munros there is an immediate boost to the ego. This natural human reaction, however, is not the prime reason a fell-runner drags his weary body across endless Munros; once again, it comes down to the challenge involved. Fell-running, like hillwalking, rock-climbing, ice-climbing or any other human endeavour, is a vibrant sport because it thrives on the physical challenge which inspired its very creation.

Many believe the appreciation of the beauty of the mountains, to be a concept alien to the fell-running fraternity. After all, how can the finer attractions and the mystical appeal of Britain's wildest country really impress its elusive charms on a lone record-breaker bashing his way through the heather to fulfil a personal quest? The truth of the matter is that in many respects the fell-runner is just as tuned in to the mountains' beauty as the hillwalker or general mountaineer. To undertake a mammoth multi-Munro marathon in a set time, whether over 24 hours or 24 days, necessitates a true devotion to running but a greater devotion to the hills. It is the hills which provide the backdrop and the inspirational spark to contemplate such a feat. If this was not the case, many fell-runners would be content with road-running and competing in city marathons.

The old adage mentioned in Chapter 3, that a true appreciation of mountain beauty is only fully reached in conjunction with sustained physical effort, is certainly applicable to the sport of fell-running. Contrary to the widely held belief that fell-runners are in the main unreceptive to the mountains' mystical allure, the exact opposite would appear to be the case, judging by the day-to-day accounts of participants of the sport. On reading about Hugh Symonds's experiences in *Running High*, for instance, one cannot fail to recognise his real passion and love for the hills, which together with the challenge they presented to him formed the twin sparks which ignited the subsequent venture. Hugh and other runners often talk of reaching a 'high' when running, almost akin to floating along with the body and mind in a state of transcendental composure, the legs seemingly doing their job effortlessly and unconsciously. During these periods the mind becomes a highly receptive vessel, and the ever-changing landscape and light patterns acquire an ethereal presence impinging on the mind with indelible intensity.

During the long night sections of the 24-hour rounds there is also much of which the daytime hillwalker is unaware. The bronze sun slowly sinking behind the serrated ridges of the west, the dancing phosphorescent colours of the northern lights shimmering against a star-lit sky, the full moon rising and picking out the silvery threads of mountain streams, and the pale glow of dawn revealing a tangle of peaks and mist-filled glens as yet untouched by the first rays of the new sun. These are images which the runner may be only dimly aware of at the time but inevitably form a lasting impression on the mind. The whole question of why people go to the hills at all will be discussed at length in Chapter 8, but it is to be hoped that this chapter has gone some way to explaining the deeds and motives of the modern-day fell-runner.

- In the summer of 1994, retired psychologist Mike Cudahy accomplished a purely self-propelled round of the Munros (no bike used) in a time of 66 days and 7 hours. However, he did use ferries to both Mull and Skye.

CHAPTER 6

One Man's Munros

Only a hill, but all of life to me,
Up there between the sunset and the sea.

Geoffrey Winthrop Young

Glancing down the long list of Munroists in the latest edition of Munro's Tables creates a distinct feeling of remote impersonality. Who are all these people? What are they doing now? Behind each and every name lies a wealth of experiences gradually acquired in the process of climbing the Munros. For a select few on the list, these experiences become known to a wider public, while the vast majority lie hidden away in memories, or more permanently as photographs, slides and notes kept in diaries or exercise books tucked away on dusty shelves.

Many of the experiences of 'the few', notably the Revd A.E. Robertson (1), Hamish M. Brown (62), Richard Gilbert (101), Chris Townsend (251), Martin Moran (383), Craig Caldwell (451), and Hugh Symonds (777), are reasonably well documented in various sources, and the bulk of these names will be familiar to anyone having read the first five chapters of this book. It is evident also that the majority of these Munroists achieved important 'firsts' – the first round of all the Munros, the first continuous round, the first round in winter, etc.

But what about the vast majority who have achieved no notable firsts? What about the average, conventional Munro-bagger who has snatched the odd weekend and holiday here and there to complete his or her Munros in the average ten years? Munroist number 594 is one such person – me. Having said this, I still don't feel I represent the average Munroist. I am probably luckier than most because I spent a great deal of my 'Munro years' in the Highlands, with the added bonus of much free time.

In common with many others, my first Munro was the great southerly eminence of Ben Lomond, standing proud on the 'bonnie banks', its fine profile enticing the novice hillwalker to reach the summit and embark on a memorable career of peak-bagging. Its close proximity to the Central Belt

Sunset on Beinn
Alligin high above
Loch Torridon

First and last: the
author on the
summit of Ben
Lomond
(11 June 1978) and
on the summit of
Ben More on Mull
(16 August 1988)

A popular first
Munro: Ben
Lomond from
Loch Ard

A Torridonian trio:
Liathach and Beinn
Eighe from Beinn
Alligin

The Five Sisters of
Kintail from Mam
Ratagan

Fort Augustus
Abbey schoolboys
camping high on
the Five Sisters
Ridge
(see Chapter 6)

Sgurr nan Gillean,
Skye

Sunset from the
Cuillin Ridge

Camasunary,
Skye

ABOVE TOP: New Year at Camasunary Bothy,
   1985–86 (see Chapter 6)
ABOVE MIDDLE: 'Fun and fresh air' on Skye:
   the south ridge of Bla Bheinn, with the
   main Cuillin Ridge behind (see Chapter 8)
ABOVE: 'Adventure and challenge': snow on
   the Cuillin Ridge in May. The Bhasteir
   Tooth and Am Basteir are behind
   (see Chapter 8)

'Beauty of the hills':
the view from
Spidean Mialach
along Loch Quoich
to Sgurr na Ciche
(see Chapter 8)

Liathach from
Loch Clair

'The mystical allure': a stunning winter's day on Meall Buidhe, Glen Lyon, looking towards distant Ben Lui (see Chapter 8)

On Beinn Dorain looking towards Ben Lui

'The mystical allure': the 'twin Buachailles' rising snow-capped and pristine from early morning valley mist

Descending Ben Lawers in low evening sun

and its position in one of the most scenic and highly publicised parts of Scotland have produced an endless flow of tourists flocking like sheep up the well-trodden path on its southern flanks. Becoming lost on Ben Lomond is difficult – it is an ideal first Munro.

Most people are introduced to hillwalking through, for example, a club, a friend, a spouse or a father, and there cannot be many instances of complete beginners deciding to climb a Munro unaccompanied. On 11 June 1978 a friend and I drove through the industrial heartland of Scotland to eventually stand atop the most southerly Munro. The word 'Munro' had not even entered my vocabulary at that time, but the event, unbeknown to me then, marked the symbolic beginning of an activity which was to assume the utmost importance in my life.

The ascent of Ben Lomond must have stirred some deep-rooted passion within me because later on that same year I found myself booked into a backpacking course based at Glenmore Lodge, the cradle of formative mountaineering years for many an experienced hill-goer. In retrospect, the course semed more like a good excuse to 'bag' as many as possible of the fairly remote Munros lying between Ben Alder and Ben Nevis in the central Highlands. Ben Alder itself is a vast, sprawling mountain lying in the heart of central Scotland's wildest area, the very antithesis of homely, easy, touristy Ben Lomond. It was certainly an unusual second Munro, by anyone's standards.

The week's course took our disparate group westwards to Loch Ossian and round the southern end of Loch Treig, where we climbed the two Munros of Stob Coire Easain and Stob a' Choire Mheadhoin. It was somewhere along the shattered quartzite grey Corries Ridge the following day that the word 'Munro' entered my consciousness, and I caught the bug. In the varied group of students, teachers, salesmen, businessmen and a headmaster there was one broad Lancastrian who had notched up an amazing 80 Munros – as he informed me nonchalantly on the ridge. My puzzled expression brought forth an explanation, and a quick calculation showed that I had climbed a meagre six Munros. Thereafter, as we stumbled along in the mist, every top we traversed was accompanied by the desperate cry, 'Is this a Munro?' – I was stricken with acute Munroitis.

On the final day of the course we traversed the fine rocky knife-edge slung between Carn Mor Dearg and the reigning (or should it be raining?) peak of Ben Nevis, my twelfth Munro. It mattered little that on the majority of these Munros there had been thick mist and no view; the mountains had called and their message was clear.

Perhaps the most significant event of 1978 in terms of my ongoing initiation was the shift from the languid, uninspiring Central Belt of Scotland to a village in the heart of the Highlands. A mathematics teacher by profession, I applied for an advertised post at St Benedict's Abbey School, Fort Augustus, the application being made *before* my June climb of Ben Lomond and therefore before I had become smitten with the mountains. It was almost as if there was a divine calling from the Highland hills which had channelled itself through the deeply spiritual and religious focus of Fort Augustus, itself the home of Scotland's oldest Benedictine community. It is fitting that the religious focus is also a physical focus, Fort Augustus occupying the geographical centre of the Highlands. Situated on the southern shore of Loch Ness, halfway along the Great Glen, which in turn divides the Grampians from the north-west Highlands, Fort Augustus has a central and unique position, and a highly enviable one for the exploration of Scotland's mountains.

The sight of marching cadets and the sound of boots on tarmac rang an incongruous and discordant note in such peaceful and monastic surroundings, or so I thought as I entered the Abbey school for the first time in May 1978 to be interviewed by the headmaster. After being led through endless corridors by a tiny first-former I met the man who an hour later offered me the post of mathematics master – and, more than that, a quality of life to which I was more than glad to become accustomed.

The idea of a cloistered, monastic existence which a school such as this conjures up is a fallacy, and in reality the Abbey school opened the door to

Mike Haines and
Fort Augustus
Abbey schoolboys
in Glen Cannich

a new and more meaningful life; in effect it has become the hub about which the rest of my life has revolved.

Not surprisingly, it wasn't long before I played an active part in the regular hillwalking trips which took place on roughly every second or third Sunday. These were initially organised by the history master, Mike Haines, whose passionate enthusiasm for the mountains was passed on to many boys, and also to me. Mike was a highly respected and devoted member of the teaching profession and an unassuming pillar of silent strength in the school. He was the definitive 'to-serve-them-all-my-days' public-school master who dedicated his life to helping and guiding young people through the turbulent years of adolescence. Mike had been a co-founder, history master and house master at the remote Rannoch School, run according to the principles of Kurt Hahn, as at Gordonstoun. Instilling a sense of adventure and qualities of maturity, independence and leadership seemed just as, if not more important than the mere acquisition of academic facts.

Mike's hillwalking trips during my first few years at the Abbey school had an almost cult following among a select few. In winter, the quick-descent technique known as glissading became the almost overriding reason for climbing a hill, and the following quote by Mike from the school newsletter in March 1979 serves to illustrate this and gives a splendid snippet of his unique character and wit.

> A much-favoured ploy on descents is to glissade on one's seat for a time, riding a mass of snow blocks yet gradually being engulfed by them. Great skill was shown by all, particularly Hell-Diver Dempster, Flying Bedstead MacCallum and the original Avalanche, Keegan, while King, Queen and O'Donoghue added their more sober cries to the general racket.

Bill Houlsby at the summit of Sgurr a'Bhealaich Dheirg, North Glen Shiel Ridge

Many of these early stravaigings took place in Glen Shiel, with its soaring, lofty ridges, such as the celebrated Five Sisters of Kintail and the South Cluanie Ridge with its seven Munros providing easy pickings for the ardent peak-bagger. I remember first looking at OS sheet 33 (Loch Alsh and Glen Shiel) with its mouthwatering concentration of Munros on either side of the glen, and thinking that this wonderland lay hardly 30 miles from Fort Augustus – a score of Munros less than an hour from home. On reflection, I suppose I cut my teeth on the Glen Shiel hills, especially in winter, and they have been the scene of some of my happiest, most carefree hill days.

I recall rising at 6 a.m. one dark October morning and setting off with a colleague (the late and sadly missed Bill Houlsby) to traverse the Five Sisters Ridge. The sight of the sun rising over the mountains marked the beginning of a truly magnificent day on the high tops. Less than a year later, in the summer of 1980, I enjoyed the profound experience of watching a Highland sunset from a high-level camp on the same ridge with four pupils. From our high perch just below Sgurr na Moraich, the most westerly peak of the Sisters, we watched in awe as the soft Highland evening light faded slowly into pale yellow and orange and finally into glorious emblazoned red behind the stark and jagged profile of the Skye Cuillin – where more dreams had yet to become reality. Varied scents and sounds were carried easily in the still evening air: bog myrtle, pines, even the smell of the sea from Loch Duich, and the shrill, haunting cry of a curlew. A more delectable camp-site could not have been found. We even had our own natural fridge of a pocket of old snow to keep the milk fresh until morning. Next day, we traversed the ridge in brilliant sunshine in slightly longer time then usual as one boy let his rucksack accidentally fall 1,000 feet into a corrie.

On another occasion, in predictably poorer weather, I was staying with a group of boys in the remote Camban Bothy just north of Glen Shiel at the head of Glen Affric. Our sights were set on Sgurr nan Ceathreamhnan, a fine Munro set in the heart of beautifully wild country. In an attempt to light a fire with damp wood, even the resourceful enthusiasm of youth failed to produce any flicker of flame. One enterprising soul stood drenched at the door after collecting a carrier-bag full of wet peat, insisting that it would do the trick. The nearest we got to a roaring fire was a room full of peaty black smoke. During the night the depressing patter of rain on the corrugated-iron bothy roof subsided to be replaced by the most haunting and poignant sound that the lonely Scottish glens can produce – the wild and eerie cry of stags during the autumn rut. The following day we abandoned our original plan but nevertheless managed a fine north-south traverse of Mullach Fraoch-choire and A'Chralaig lying north of Loch Cluanie.

Although there were school trips to other areas, such as the Mamores, Creag Meagaidh and Glen Affric, it was always Glen Shiel that we returned to again and again. In May 1979, Bill Houlsby and I made our first foray to the hills surrounding Glencoe, climbing the prominent Pap of Glencoe and its continuation to the Munro of Sgor nam Fiannaidh, the end peak of Aonach Eagach, the conspicuous 'notched ridge' on the north side of the glen. The sight of the rocky crest with its twists, turns and airy pinnacles provoked an overwhelming desire within me to traverse the ridge, and just over a week later I took up the challenge. Besides being the first real scrambling that I had ever done, the outing was notable on another count: Meall Dearg (the other Munro on the ridge) was the first Munro I had climbed completely on my own, and marked the beginning of many other solo trips. Solitary hillwalking I find to be a more intense and powerful experience than with companions, and the extra vigilance required nurtures a keener and sharper perception of the surroundings.

The traverse of the rocky spine of Aonach Eagach brought a physical release of my latent scrambling tendencies and I revelled in and relished the exhilaration of co-ordinated movement on steep, dry rock, with numerous hand and footholds of course. My diary for that day ends with the words 'next stop the Cuillin Ridge!', and spring 1980 saw my first introduction to Britain's finest range of mountains.

For many newcomers to Skye, the bold tapering spire of Sgurr nan Gillean is usually the first peak to be seen as one rounds the last bend to the isolated oasis of the Slighachan Hotel. It is also very often the first of the Cuillin peaks to be climbed, by the somewhat inappropriately named 'tourist route'. This was the mountain and intended route which I had planned for 19 April 1980, and it was yet another solo venture. W.A. Poucher's dramatic descriptions of the Cuillin Ridge in his book *The Scottish Peaks* had fired my imagination but had also impressed on me the dangers for inexperienced climbers on these steep, rocky and often mist-shrouded summits. I was aware that many mountain accidents are caused by climbers attempting routes beyond their limitations, but having found no real difficulty on Aonach Eagach I certainly believed the tourist route on Sgurr Nan Gillean to be well within my scope. However, whether it was because I hadn't read the guide-book properly or maybe the map was upside down, I eventually found myself on Bealach Bhasteir, the col between Sgurr Nan Gillean and Am Basteir, staring up at the unknown, pinnacled complexities of the west ridge. I subsequently learned that the west ridge of Sgurr Nan Gillean was a Moderate rock climb and no place for novice scramblers. Yet here I was, on my inaugural trip to the most dangerous mountain range in Great Britain, about to embark on a solo climb up one of the trickier sections of the Cuillin Ridge! Those familiar with this ridge will remember that 1980 was seven years before the extremely awkward pinnacle known as 'the Gendarme' disappeared, thereby removing the crux of the entire route. I distinctly remember coming face to face with this grim obstruction and the awful realisation that I was indeed on the 'wrong' ridge. The remarkable three-metre high obelisk rose directly in front of me on a water-thin section of ridge with yawning drops on either side. Having just climbed a steep gully on polished rock which I had no intention of descending, there only remained the option of attempting to by-pass the offending 'policeman'. Easily said, but the aerial ballet and desperately exposed antics required to circumvent this thankfully deceased obstruction remain a vivid and sober reminder of the fine dividing line between life and death.

The remainder of the west ridge offers delightful scrambling and the narrow summit of Sgurr nan Gillean must be one of the finest viewpoints in Scotland. Blaven's magnificent profile is seen to perfection, while the main

Cuillin Ridge stretches in a twisting but unbroken chain of peaks, pinnacles and passes to Gars-Bheinn at the southern end of the ridge. The more rounded outline of the Red Cuillin provides a perfect contrast to this jagged skyline, and the surrounding seascape of azure blue backed by the hazy outline of the Outer Hebrides forms a splendid backdrop to this glorious scene. Not surprisingly, Sgurr nan Gillean has over the years become my favourite Munro, and I made my tenth ascent in the summer of 1992.

The brash inexperience of youth was further displayed on that first attempt when I *descended* the west ridge in order to 'bag' the neighbouring Munro of Am Basteir.

I made my second ascent of Sgur nan Gillean in the summer of 1981 with a group of boys from the Abbey school, only this time I did succeed in locating the tourist route. My three aspiring Alpinists revelled in the airy scramble on rough, sun-kissed gabbro and seemed genuinely disappointed to reach the summit because they had so enjoyed the climb. In fact, one of the boys (a German) was so enthralled by his Skye weekend that on prize day that year his parents presented me with a bottle of best German wine to thank me for making his trip so memorable. They didn't mention his maths results!

It was also in the summer of 1981 that I made my first ascent of the 'ultimate Munro', the Inaccessible Pinnacle. In terms of technical difficulty this is certainly the hardest Munro, requiring a Moderate rock climb to reach the exposed and airy summit. The In. Pin. forms part of the classic 'Round of Coire Lagan' and I had already become acquainted with Sgurr Alasdair and Sgurr Mhic Coinnich, two other Munros on this grand traverse. Fortunately, I met up with a group of people who kindly offered me their rope to effect the necessary abseil off the summit. The whole experience was so enjoyable that I promptly made a second ascent followed by another abseil.

During the long nine-week summer holiday of 1981 the realisation that I had completed nearly 80 Munros gave me the necessary impetus to attempt to reach the magic 100 before the new term began in mid-September. For two glorious weeks I drove round the north-western Highlands picking off succulent fruits such as Liathach, Beinn Alligin, An Teallach and Ben Hope. I had begun in Skye with the three Munros in the central section of the ridge and completed the Cuillin with Bruach na Frithe, ironically the easiest Munro on the whole ridge.

The hardest Munro: the Inaccessible Pinnacle of Sgurr Dearg, Skye

On leaving Skye, bad luck took over as I ripped a car tyre on the metal runner on the ferry. As I erected the tent in Glen Torridon the same day, I was reduced to a quivering wreck by clouds of midges. Lying in the tent later I heard a scratching and gnawing sound at my side and immediately shone the torch to discover a thumb-sized hole in the fabric of the tent.

A rodent, probably a rat, had gnawed through the tent! Not only that; clouds of midges were now entering the hole for a midnight feast. In a final gesture of exasperated outrage I dismantled the tent and spent an uncomfortable, but midge-and-rat-free night on the back seat of the car.

The following day marked the beginning of a heatwave that was to last for over a week, during which I enjoyed a magnificent traverse of Liathach. During the climb I met up with two other keen hillwalkers who informed me that Liathach, previously containing only one Munro, now boasted two, due to a recent revision of Munro's Tables. An Teallach, a mountain I intended to climb in a few days' time, they also informed me had doubled its Munro count from one to two. Quite frankly, at the time I thought that they were pulling a fast one. After all, who apart from Sir Hugh himself could have the authority to tamper with the sacred Tables? However, a visit to Torridon post office/shop that same day reliably confirmed their information when I purchased a copy of the latest Munro's Tables complete with the controversial Donaldson Brown revisions. (The issue of the 'rights and wrongs' of those and other changes to the list of Munros is discussed more fully in Appendix 1.)

On the ridge that day I also met another maths teacher by the name of John Burgess, who taught in London although his love of the Scottish mountains was so great that he was desperate for a teaching post north of the Border. He positively drooled with envy when I told him of my job at Fort Augustus! Four years later he was teaching at Strathallan school in Perthshire and I had just moved to Kilgraston school, only three miles from Strathallan. Not surprisingly, we met in a local pub and have since made numerous expeditions together.

For the next few days I made the best of the heatwave with ascents of Beinn Alligin, An Teallach and the longest day I had yet had on the hills, climbing seven Munros in the Fannichs range, bringing my tally to 94. A vague notion of trying to make the most northerly Munro, Ben Hope, my 100th did not materialise – it was, in fact, my 97th, after the twin quartzite peaks of Ben More Assynt and Conival. The hot, hazy and muggy weather which accompanied me on Ben Hope was a sign that the heatwave was ending, and indeed the forecast for the following day was not good. However, I was determined to top my 100th Munro the next day and I left my base at the Ullapool camp-site at 7.20 a.m., heading for the Beinn Dearg group of Munros lying south-east of Ullapool in the Inverlael Forest. The three compact hills of Meall nan Ceapraichean, Cona Mheall and Beinn Dearg were climbed in wet, windy and misty conditions with the hundredth Munro of Beinn Dearg something of an anticlimax.

In retrospect, this was a watershed in my Munro-bagging career. For various reasons climbing Munros took a back seat for the next year or two, and it was in fact nearly seven months before I climbed another new Munro. It was as if the wind had gone out of my sails after the 100th, and certainly the early Eighties (from August 1981) were a slack time.

However, on 31 May 1982 during half-term an ambition of mine finally reached maturity when I accomplished a one-day traverse of the Cuillin Ridge on Skye. I had discovered scrambling routes to have enormous personal appeal and the idea of linking the 11 Munros of the Black Cuillin in a single outing captured my imagination to the point of obsession. I also felt that the necessary preparation had been done, having already climbed all the Cuillin Munros and even descended the east ridge of the Inaccessible Pinnacle, which is necessary if a rope is not carried to abseil off the steep west ridge.

The adventure began the previous day as I made the long trudge to reach the southern end of the ridge, where I bivouacked near the summit of Sgurr nan Eag, the first Munro of the traverse. As the sun dropped behind the ink-black outline of the ridge, I lay in my sleeping-bag on a rocky ledge poised on the threshold of what I hoped would be a successful venture. Sleep never really came, and by 4.30 a.m. I was standing on the summit of Sgurr nan Eag watching the first rays of the sun tinting the ridge with an orange light. Eleven hours later I stood on the summit of Sgurr nan Gillean following a perfect traverse in perfect conditions. That night, while staying in the Sligachan Hotel, I was amazed to meet the late Walter Poucher, author of *The Scottish Peaks* and *The Magic of Skye*, my copy of the latter book being duly signed by him.

The next major turning point in my 'Munro memoirs' came in the summer of 1985, when I finally moved south from the Highland haven of Fort Augustus to teach at Kilgraston school in Bridge of Earn, Perthshire. Prior to this, the Abbey school had been going through a rough patch, and its closure due to falling rolls had been announced in the summer of 1985. The creation of an 'action committee', however, temporarily prevented the intended shutdown, but eight years later, in 1993, the school's fate was finally sealed, when its doors closed for the last time. The years preceding 1985 had seen an exodus of some of the best teachers, two of whom now teach at Strathallan school just 'up the road' from Kilgraston.

At the time of the move I had completed 140 Munros – just over halfway – and was determined that my migration southwards would not interfere with their intended completion. In fact, quite the contrary turned out to be the case. Perthshire has dozens of Munros, few of which I had climbed, and I had not even touched the huge mass of the Cairngorms. The Tilt, the Tarff and the Mounth contained further unfrequented territory with a host of new peaks. Quite simply, I was in an ideal situation to claim most of the Munros I had yet to do, and just over a year later, in October

1986, I climbed Mount Keen, the most easterly Munro and my 200th. In little over a year since moving to Perthshire I had climbed 60 Munros. In the last *four* years of my time at Fort Augustus I had only managed 40. From a Munro-bagging perspective the shift to Perthshire had been almost as fruitful as the initial move to Inverness-shire.

The 1985 watershed initiated an annual event that has since attracted an almost cult following among a few of my hillwalking friends. Spending the New Year in a bothy was something I hadn't even thought about until John Burgess (remember Liathach?) firmly fixed the notion in my head over a few beers.

Camasunary Bothy on Skye, with its magnificent position on the wild and remote shores of the bay which gives it its name, was the intended venue for Hogmanay 1985. Lying at the foot of the long south ridge of Blaven and directly below the dramatic Cuillin viewpoint of Sgurr na Stri, with good sea views of Rum, it occupies an almost ideally romantic position.

Five of us spent a memorable three nights there to see in New Year 1986. Three of the party, including me, had connections with the Abbey school – two of us teachers (myself and Ian Keith) and one an ex-pupil, Gavin Queen, who, like me, spent his formative hillwalking years at Fort Augustus. Although everything had to be carried in, no expense was spared – and coal for the fire was the most awkward and bulky item to carry. Driftwood was plentiful so we had a blazing fire each night, quite the most important thing in a bothy at this time of year. With darkness falling by 5 p.m., it is a long night, but with good company, a roaring fire and plenty to eat and drink the time inevitably flies. A canny ploy on such a winter's evening is to stretch out the dinner courses, or rather the time between them, so that the pleasurable act of eating (and drinking!) becomes the focus of the whole evening. A typical dinner at the bothy could last up to five hours and consist of around eight courses.

On returning to the bothy after a day on the hill, we would usually start with a warming mug of tea and a mince pie. This would be followed some time later by the first dram of the evening. The meal proper consisted of soup, a main course with wine, Christmas pudding and brandy sauce, a selection of cheese and biscuits followed by port, coffee and mints, Christmas cake and another dram. This stage was usually reached by about ten o'clock, which still left plenty of time to engage in some serious drinking and merry-making.

New Year 1986 at Camasunary set the scene for subsequent similar occasions, and in fact it was decided there and then that every other Hogmanay would be spent at Camasunary, with other bothies being tried in intervening years. However, Camasunary always held its fascination and romantic appeal. A run of five 'bothy New Years' was made before the

custom temporarily ceased for two (more traditional) New Years, only to be followed by a more grandiose plan in 1992.

Lying close to the bothy at Camasunary is a large, privately owned lodge, which through a complex series of events I managed to rent for a week in the summer of 1992. A dozen of us revelled in the peace and solitude of a remote Highland outpost, enjoying to the full the walking, climbing, fishing and boating, and the use of a Land Rover. Six months later a group of us returned to spend New Year there, accompanied by abysmally wet and windy weather but armed to the teeth with all the trappings of a real Hogmanay celebration. On Hogmanay itself, ten of us sat round a solid teak table in formal dress eating roast turkey and trimmings – the following night we found more room for venison and pheasant. This was all washed down with copious quantities of wine, whisky, port, beer and anything else available!

These New Year episodes serve to illustrate how the act of Munro-bagging can lead on directly and indirectly to deeper and richer experiences. The climbing of Munros places the individual on a

Camasunary Bothy (left) and Lodge (right). The Munro of Bla Bheinn rises behind

107

springboard to a deeper appreciation of nature, himself and his relationship to others, and in the end this is all that really matters.

One more rewarding experience is worth briefly narrating before concluding this chapter with an account of my last Munro experience. In the summer of 1987 I was persuaded by a friend to accompany him on a continuous traverse of all eight 4,000-foot peaks in Scotland. This challenge was established by the Rucksack Club in 1954 and subsequently became a 24-hour challenge for fell-runners, as mentioned in Chapter 5. Our target was to cover the 85 miles and 17,000 feet of ascent in four days. The main aim of the venture was to raise money for a local charity, as well as providing a worthwhile challenge. Light rucksacks were carried, with heavier overnight gear, such as sleeping-bags and stoves, deposited at the overnight stopping points by a support party.

Myself and the main support person (John Burgess) decided to climb Ben Nevis (the first 4,000-footer of the trip) the day before the official start in order to savour the unique experience of bivouacking atop the highest peak in Britain. In theory, this sounded like a good idea, except that our proposed route of ascent was Tower Ridge, a Difficult rock climb on the north face of the mountain. In fact, in good summer weather the route should be well within the limits of experienced mountaineers and even determined scramblers, provided a rope is carried.

However, a 6 p.m. start with mist low on the mountain and heavy packs did not bode well. Halfway up the ridge we found ourselves floundering on steep, slabby and greasy rock, and both of us knew we had wandered off-route, having completed it previously in clear weather. After resorting to sack-hauling with the rope, one of the sacks managed to dislodge a massive chunk of rock, which peeled away from the face and disappeared into the misty depths below. We did not reach the summit shelter until 11 p.m.

During the early hours of the next morning the mist cleared on the summit to reveal a staggeringly beautiful dawn, with fleecy cumulus cloud stretching below us to the horizon, and the chirp, chirping of a snow bunting welcoming the new day. Simon Pengelley, the organiser of the four-day expedition, did not arrive on the summit of Ben Nevis until 11 a.m. after leaving Fort William in low-lying cloud and flogging up the tourist path to emerge into bright sunshine on the summit.

Our real venture then began in earnest as we made our way down along the narrow crest of the Carn Mor Dearg arête to start our traverse of the remaining Nevis 4,000-footers of Carn Mor Dearg, Aonach Mor and Aonach Beag. Our destination that night was Loch Ossian Youth Hostel, almost 20 miles from Ben Nevis, and which we finally reached at 10 p.m.

The following day was the easiest of the four, consisting 'only' of a 22-mile cross-country trek to the dreary outpost of Dalwhinnie, the halfway point of the trip. Our normally efficient back-up man, John Burgess, who had decided to bag the two Munros to the south-east of Loch Ossian, was not there when we arrived, and two hours later, after negotiating our way into the Ben Alder transport café for a meal and beds, we were genuinely worried that he had perhaps had an accident. In fact, he had misread the train timetable at the youth hostel!

Our intended destination for the third day was Glen Feshie and the Ruig-aiteachain Bothy, a shorter day than the previous one but 'against the grain' of the country, with much heather-plodding, stream-crossing and cursing. This left us poised for the difficult fourth day, involving a traverse of all four Cairngorm 4,000-footers. The previous three days had been bright and sunny, but our final day was one of difficult compass navigation in clammy mist as we staggered round the featureless plateau which forms much of the high country in the Cairngorms. After the traverse of Cairn Toul and Braeriach, the steep climb out of the glacial trough of the Lairig Ghru was exhausting, but only Ben MacDui and Cairn Gorm remained to complete the trip.

Twelve hours after leaving the bothy and four days after my nightmare ascent of Tower Ridge on Ben Nevis, we stood on the summit of Cairn Gorm and shook each other's hands. Having completed a route such as this brings home the full enormity of Martin Stone's incredible time of 21 hours 31 minutes for the same route. As far as I am concerned, his record was pretty safe! However, the completion of the route in our 'leisurely' four days

The author (right) and John Burgess above the clouds on the summit of Ben Nevis, before the four-day traverse of Scotland's 4,000-foot peaks

brought immense satisfaction, and the fact that we had raised money for a good cause was an added bonus.

At the time of this challenge I had less than 50 Munros left to climb, and I was realistically looking a year hence to the summer of 1988 for the date of their intended completion. This would imply an average of about one Munro a week for the next year, which, weather permitting, was a viable proposition. However, the remainder were a diverse collection of mostly remote or fairly inaccessible hills which would require a disciplined, co-ordinated approach to complete in the time available.

A case in point is a weekend in May 1988 when I climbed four extremely remote Munros in the area of Geldie Lodge, south of the Cairngorms. I had walked seven miles from Linn of Dee near Braemar to make camp just short of Geldie Lodge. I then proceeded to head north over rough heather and peat hags to claim the two rounded summits of Beinn Bhrotain and Monadh Mor, the latter being my 250th Munro. At 8.30 p.m. I was back at the tent, only to be up and off again at 6.45 the next morning, heading south this time to the two heather domes of An Sgarsach and Carn an Fhidhleir, the latter vying with A'Mhaighdean in the Fisherfield forest as the remotest Munro, and one of the three not climbed by Sir Hugh Munro. (Incidentally, I didn't climb A'Mhaighdean until July of that year.) The end of this particular skirmish left 25 Munros still to do, and various Duke of Edinburgh Award commitments at school along with other engagements meant that it was two months before I was able to tackle these last few.

At the beginning of 1988 I had booked a cottage on Mull for a week in mid-August in order to provide my base for an ascent of Ben More, the only island Munro outside Skye and the most popular 'last Munro' for this very reason. Those who remember the summer of 1988 will possibly also remember the claims that July that year was one of the wettest since records began, and this was the month that I stumbled and squelched my way round 23 of the most disparate Munros, clocking up over 1,000 miles in the car and almost 200 on foot. These ranged from obscure, featureless Cairngorm lumps to the wet and wild peaks of Knoydart, and further north to the rugged, remote summits of the Fisherfield forest and still further north to the isolated sentinel of Ben Klibreck in Sutherland. That final three-week peak-bagging spree was a microcosm of the last ten years. There was rain (an understatement), wind, midges and clammy, compass-guided mist wanderings, but there was also euphoric, sun-kissed ridge scrambling, glorious sunsets and happy encounters with like-minded hill-goers.

That memorable July odyssey had left just two unclimbed Munros: Ben More on Mull and an isolated Cairngorm peak called Bynack More, which I planned to do with friends at the beginning of August, making it

my last mainland Munro. The penultimate Munro would not appear to be the cause of any great celebration, but when my only walking companion, Gavin Queen, produced a bottle of champagne from his rucksack on the summit I immediately thought otherwise. Now if you celebrate with one bottle of champagne on your second-last Munro, I suppose you must go one further on the last.

So on 16 August 1988 five of us lay sprawled around the trig-point on the summit of Ben More sharing two bottles of bubbly to the amused bewilderment of the few other walkers. We had just ascended the north-east ridge from the subsidiary top of A'Choich, the only real scrambling route on the mountain. Narrowing almost to a knife-edge in places, it provided a fitting end to an era. Ben More epitomises the romantic ideal of everything a mountain should have: a narrow, rocky ridge leading to a finely tapered summit, grand sea views and an air of remoteness true to its island locality. We were also lucky in having chosen the only decent day in a week of rather wet and windy weather.

Hardly any time after reaching the summit, the inevitable period of reflection began to set in. Completing the Munros is almost like losing a good friend. Their perpetual challenge over many years gives life a richer meaning, way above the humdrum of everyday existence. In an instant this challenge is no more, and a constant and faithful companion for ten years

The end of an era: leaving the summit of the author's last Munro, Ben More on Mull

has disappeared with the sunset. Feelings of euphoria soon become tinged with sadness, and it is not uncommon for some Munroists to suffer acute depression after completion.

In my own case, I was fortunate enough to realise that Munros are not the only challenge in Scotland, although they had certainly dominated my leisure time over the previous ten years. Exactly a week after that triumphant day on Mull, I climbed 2,882-foot Ben Ledi near Callander, a superb little peak with excellent views and only an hour's drive from my home in Perthshire – and I hadn't even climbed it before. Why? Because it fell 118 feet short of that magical height. Ben Ledi is a Corbett, as are such distinguished peaks as Beinn Resipol, Rois-Bheinn, Streap, Ben Aden, Beinn Dearg Mor, Cul Mor, Canisp, Quinag and Beinn Loyal; all those and many more I had yet to climb. On completing the Munros, I had only climbed 13 of the 221 Corbetts, so there were still plenty of new challenges and grand hill days to come. There were also the remaining 3,000-foot Tops in Scotland, together with the other 3,000-footers in the rest of Britain and Ireland. In 1992 an idea of mine to classify the best scrambling routes in Scotland finally culminated in the publication of *Classic Mountain Scrambles in Scotland* (Mainstream). A second idea of undertaking a marathon backpack through the Highlands of Scotland culminated in a four-week charity hike from the Mull of Kintyre lighthouse to Cape Wrath lighthouse in July 1989, one of the most satisfying and stimulating periods of my life. (Post-Munro activities are discussed more fully in Chapter 9.)

I hope that this chapter has gone some way in explaining the psyche of the common Munro-bagger, and the experiences of Munroist number 594 described here, though unique, are roughly representative of the thousand others in the list. It is worth noting that this chapter could be written a thousand times by other Munroists, each describing their own set of experiences, each climbing the same Munros, yet each account being as unique as the writer's own fingerprint. That is the beauty of the Munros: they offer everything to everyone, and every day on the hill is subtly different, even when doing the same Munro again. The variety and combinations of route, weather, mood, companions and season are virtually infinite, and the Munros themselves provide only the basic framework about which we clothe our rich tapestry of personal experiences. Completing the Munros is not the end; it is only the beginning.

CHAPTER 7

The Lighter Side

Tam the Bagger

When Munro machos leave the street,
And couthybaggers baggers meet,
As mountain-days are wearing late,
An' sufferin' spouses wait – irate;
While we sit dreamin' at the cairn,
Of no' hae'n a wifie and a bairn,
We think na on the lang Scots miles,
The Tops and peat hags, bogs and stiles
That lie between us and our hame
Where sits our sulky, sullen dame,
Gathering her brows like gathering storm,
Nursing her wrath to keep it warm.

(Apologies to Tam o' Shanter and Robert Burns)

According to Dave Brown and Ian Mitchell in their award-winning book *A View From the Ridge* (Ernest Press), the bulk of mountaineering literature falls neatly into one of three categories: the epic, the metaphysical or the couthy. Most Himalayan odysseys and perhaps Moran's *The Munros in Winter* and Hugh Symonds's *Running High* falls into the first category. The esoteric and philosophical observations found in the works of W.H. Murray and, to a lesser extent, Gordon Stainforth fit well into the second category. Obvious candidates for the third would be the three books of Dave Brown and Ian Mitchell, together with such classics as *Always a Little Further* by Alastair Borthwick (Diadem).

The danger of categorisation is that there will always be books which refuse to slot neatly into one genus – much of, say, Hamish Brown's or Tom Weir's work does not easily lend itself to such black-and-white categorisation. Indeed, many such books contain aspects of all three groups.

The humorous side of mountaineering is partly contained within the couthy (earthy humour) category but not all humorous mountaineering books can be described as couthy; for instance, Muriel Gray's *The First Fifty – Munro-Bagging Without a Beard* has its own special brand of humour which is hilariously down to earth but not couthy in the strict sense of the word. In general, amusing mountaineering books are thin on the ground and the only other two which immediately spring to mind are *The Ridiculous Mountains* (Tales of the Doctor and his friends among the Highland Hills) by G.J.F. Dutton and, more recently, *Nothing So Simple as Climbing* (both Diadem) and *The Ascent of Rum Doodle* by W.E. Bowman (Arrow). The first two of these are collections of amusing short stories about three characters' bizarre adventures climbing in the Scottish hills. The author is an honorary member of the Scottish Mountaineering Club, and the bulk of the stories have appeared in the *SMC Journal*. *The Ascent of Rum Doodle* is a marvellously funny satirical skit which parodies the first ascent of Everest and was published shortly after the event, in 1956.

While on the subject of satire, one outstanding contributor to the field of Scottish mountaineering literature, and in particular the humorous side, must surely be mentioned – the late Tom Patey, who was tragically killed in May 1970 while abseiling from a sea-stack off the northern Scottish coast. His *One Man's Mountains* (Gollancz) has been described by Chris Bonnington as 'the most entertaining climbing book I have ever read', and W.H. Murray called it 'the most splendid memorial that Patey could have . . . No mountain writer has ever made me laugh so much.'

In recent years, an offbeat, zany publication devoted entirely to hillwalking has been rolling off the presses every two months. The Angry Corrie (Scotland's first and best hillwalker's fanzine), edited by Dave Hewitt,* is a delightfully funny collection of articles, cartoons, letters and generally acute satirical observations about anything remotely connected with Scottish hills, and Munros in particular. Several more serious articles also help to complement the magazine's humorous bent. The stereotyped image of the lone male Munro-bagger complete with beard, glasses, woolly hat and cagoule is affectionately and amusingly portrayed in comic-strip form by the character of 'Murdo Munro' ('he's a bugger of a bagger'). The only drawback of the fanzine is that it can be quite difficult to obtain, being only available in selected outdoor shops throughout Scotland and one or two pubs, such as the Clachaig Inn, Glencoe.

---

* See also *Walking the Watershed* (Tacit Press) by Dave Hewitt, a marvellous tale of walking the great divide of Scotland

The remainder of this chapter will be spent lightheartedly examining various aspects of the Munro phenomenon, beginning with the disease itself, that of chronic Munrosis.

From the identification of the disease itself in 1901, nearly 50 years were to pass before the first ten cases were recorded and 70 years were to pass before 100 people had been known to become afflicted with the condition. The rate of growth of this rampant disease is now known to be exponential, and by the early 1990s over 1,000 people had been affected. These statistics indicate that the affliction has now reached epidemic proportions and the number of new cases is doubling roughly every seven years. At the present growth rate, it is estimated that by the year 2050 one million people could have contracted the disease, and indeed before 2080, less than 100 years from now, the entire population of Britain will be acute sufferers. It is likely then that rather than continue the list of Munroists in Munro's Tables, it will be easier to list those who have not climbed the Munros, i.e. who have not contracted the disease – the anti-Munroists. Obviously, many of these exist today, one notable case being Tom Weir, who says he wants to be the first person not to climb all the Munros.

The symptoms of chronic Munrosis reach their peak at weekends and holidays when the sufferer contracts an overwhelming and obsessive desire to elevate himself above the 3,000-foot contour, often accompanied by others also afflicted by the same mad, compulsive behaviour. An acute form of the disease is also prevalent in some individuals who are compelled to leave the crowds of 'normal' Munro-baggers and go off in search of obscure Tops. Some of these have been known to have been followed by little men in white coats, and the severe neurosis of Top-bagging often results in several months' confinement in institutions such as Creag Dunain in Inverness. A glimmer of insight into the psyche of the Top-bagger can be found by reading the madcap antics of the Doctor and his companions in the chapter 'Finishing off a Top' in *The Ridiculous Mountains* by G.J.F. Dutton.

Early symptoms of Munrosis present themselves when normally healthy, well-adjusted individuals begin to show an unhealthy interest in boots, woolly hats and GoreTex clothing. The Saturday-morning shopping trip begins to see the hen-pecked husband furtively glancing through the window of the climbing shop to the shocking but mouth-watering display of coloured ice-axes, crampons, and turquoise-and-mauve fleece jackets. Some may even take the plunge and desert their spouses in Safeway to enter the hallowed portals of this male-dominated domain. Once inside, they are immediately pounced upon by grotesquely fit, fleece-jacketed assistants who themselves have doubtlessly reached an advanced state of Munrosis. Half an hour later they surreptitiously leave with a plain carrier bag containing a pair of loop-stitch socks and a book on the Munros.

Apparently 20 minutes of sex does you as much good as climbing three Munros.

Although Munrosis is curiously predominant in the male, and particularly those with beards (beard growth often occurs in the aftermath of contracting the disease but the reason for this is unknown), an increasing number of females are also becoming afflicted. However, in the main these are the wives or girlfriends of an already affected male, and the number of incidents of lone females with the disease is surprisingly low.

Those marriages where only one partner is affected (usually the male) often begin to flounder or become seriously strained. Domestic bliss becomes severely hampered as the weekend approaches and 'Tam the Bagger' (see opening poem) spreads his OS sheet out on the living-room floor to plan his route – to the total disgust of his long-suffering spouse. Of course, many wives are more understanding of their husband's predicament and are thankful at least that he hasn't taken up pot-holing or hang-gliding. Some attempt, misguidedly, to contact support clubs such as Munro-holics Anonymous (MA) or other low-altitude therapy groups, but, well intentioned as these are, they rarely provide more than a temporary interruption to the disease's overwhelming progress.

As the annual holiday approaches, arguments inevitably ensue concerning 'the fresh air benefits' of a fourth Highland vacation (vigorously pursued by Tam) or the more conventional scenario of joining the brain-dead beached whales on the Costa Del Sol. The unavoidable conclusion to these marital altercations is separate holidays, with Tam pursuing his relentless quest in his beloved Scottish Highlands, and the wife and kids spending a memorably miserable fortnight at Loret de Mar. Thus one more nail is firmly hammered into the coffin of marital harmony. It is reckoned that by the year 2030 the majority of separations and divorces will have resulted from Munro-related addictions.

One might be forgiven for thinking that once the disease has run its natural course and all the Munros have been climbed, the sufferer readjusts to a normal lifestyle. In a few cases this is certainly true, but an alarming number of Munroists are known to suffer an extremely debilitating condition called Post-Munro Depression (PMD), or Munrosis Melancholia, which can be worse than the disease itself. In extremely severe cases, suicide can result, usually by jumping off the Inaccessible Pinnacle on Skye or Lord Berkley's Seat on An Teallach. A group of manic Munro depressives have recently set up a self-help organisation known as the Munro Samaritans, whose telephone number can be found buried in the cairns of most Munro summits.

For many, the only way to counteract the acute effects of PMD is to transfer their addictive peak-bagging tendencies to other elevations, such as Tops, Corbetts or Furth of Scotland. The variant Corbettitus is not as prevalent as Munrosis but is known only to affect those already smitten with the parent disease of Munrosis. Recurrence of the disease is also becoming more common and the condition of Secondary Munrosis often gains momentum when the Munroist realises that he or she is well into completing a second round of the Munros. The rare condition of Polymunrosis is the natural consequence of Secondary Munrosis and a growing number of authenticated cases are becoming known, in particular Munroist number 327, R. Stewart Logan, who has completed the Munros five times and the ubiquitous Hamish Brown (62), who is now known to have completed seven rounds. Such acute variants of the original disease are likely to remain a rarity, as is the even more exceptional derivative of Pure Polymunrosis, where each successive round is started from scratch. Most multiple completions documented in Munro's Tables could be said to be termed examples of Pseudo Polymunrosis. An increasingly common variant is that of Munrosis Integrale, a condition where the sufferer feels compelled to complete the round in a single expedition. The first documented case was Hamish Brown in 1974, and since then various others have followed suit.

Other extremely abormal variants are mentioned in the *SMC Journal* of 1991 including Munrosis Incrementalis – the climbing of the Munros in order of height – and Munrosis Alphabeticus – the climbing of all Munros in alphabetical order and even Munrosis Nocturnalis, the ultimate cure for insomniacs. As yet, no cases of the above conditions have come to light – unless you know otherwise?

The next chapter includes a full discussion of why people climb Munros and go to the hills generally. However, there is also the reverse consideration of why some people don't climb Munros or, rather, do climb them but don't feel up to it on certain specific occasions. Tom Patey's *One Man's Mountains* contains a hilarious collection of 'commonly used ploys' for not going climbing, in an article entitled 'The Art of Climbing Down Gracefully'. Many of these are directly applicable to Munro-baggers but it must be said that the fanatical devotion of the bagger ensures that he rarely has an off-day or a day spent at leisure with the family. From what has been said on marriage break-ups, the 'Responsible Family Man' ploy would not appear to figure much in Tam the Bagger's thinking.

The 'chossy-climb' ploy could be paralleled by the 'boring-Munro' ploy, although one well-known Munroist often likes to make the point that there are no boring Munros, only boring people. Yet all peak-baggers at some time in their career will curse quietly to themselves as they slog up and over endless heather and peat hags on any one of four Geal Charns or 18 Meall somethings and wonder what on earth they are doing there. A few of the more gullible will be temporarily numbed by the bold assertion that 'every Munro is unique' or 'every Munro has its own character', forgetting of course that some may have very little or no character at all.

This all is leading on to the theory of 'tedious Munrosis', which by a process of simple logical deduction infers that there are, in fact, no boring Munros – although it fails to throw any light on boring people. The theory makes its point by a method known as *reductio ad absurdum* – reduction to absurdity, for non-Latin scholars. The proof begins with the assumption or axiom that there do indeed exist a class of boring Munros, and hence concurrently also a class of 'not boring' Munros – we shall call these interesting Munros. The deductive reasoning will proceed until we arrive at a contradiction (or absurdity), thus negating the initial axiom and disproving the conjecture. Examples of interesting Munros include Ben Nevis (the highest), Mount Keen (the most easterly), Ben More on Mull (the only island Munro outside Skye), the Inaccessible Pinnacle (the hardest) and Ben Hope (the most northerly), i.e. Munros which possess some definable characteristic which sets them apart from the rest. Now, turning to our list of boring Munros, we can arrange them in order of 'boringness' from the most boring Munro up to the least boring. Now select the Munro from the bottom of this blacklist – the most boring Munro. Surely that is an interesting characteristic! In other words, the most boring Munro is actually interesting by the very fact that it is the most boring. We are now compelled to place this Munro in the list of interesting Munros, leaving us again with another most boring Munro. By applying the same procedure again and again we are left with no boring Munros and our initial assumption that there are some boring Munros must be wrong. Conclusion: all Munros are interesting!

Thus there is no excuse for the half-hearted Munro-bagger to leave the boring Munros until later – there are none. It is certainly true, however, that some patient hillwalkers leave *some* Munros until later in life as they cannot bear to finish, and the following poem by an anonymous author concludes this brief excursion into the lighter side of Munro-bagging:

The Old Munro Bagger

'You are old Munro-bagger,' the young man said,
'The locks that are left you are grey,
And yet you go on bagging tops all the time,
Now give me the reason I pray.'

'In the days of my youth,' Munro-bagger replied,
'I remembered that youth would fly past,
And abused not my health and my vigour at first,
That I might go on right up to the last.'

'You are old Munro-bagger,' the young man said,
'And pleasures with youth pass away,
And yet you lament not the hills that are done,
Now give me the reason I pray.'

'In the days of my youth,' Munro-bagger replied,
'I remembered that youth could not last,
So I saved up some hills that I could have done then,
To do them when life's nearly past.'

'You are old Munro-bagger,' the young man cried,
'There are some you still have to do,
If death comes first as you know that it might,
Whatever will come of the few?'

'I am cheerful young man,' Munro-bagger replied,
'Some day you will understand too,
The challenge is not in the ones you have done,
But in those that you still have to do.'

'I am patient young man,' Munro-bagger said,
'For I have enjoyed a long life through;
It is not the ones left that are keeping me going
But the new ones they are making me do.'

A few Munro-baggers will go to extraordinary lengths to disguise themselves on the hill

CHAPTER 8

The Why of it All

Why climb the mountains? I will tell you why,
And if my fancy jumps not with your whim,
What marvel? There is scope beneath the sky
For things that creep, and fly, and walk, and swim.
I love the free breath of the broad-wing'd breeze,
I love the free bird poised at lofty ease,
And the free torrents far-upsounding hymn;
I love to leave my littleness behind
In the low vale where little cares are great,
And in the mighty map of things to find
A sober measure of my scanty state,
Taught by the vastness of God's pictured plan
In the big world how small a thing is man!
John Stuart Blackie, 'How Small is Man'

On returning from a day on the hills recently, a non-hillwalking friend of mine iterated that he 'would quite like to join me on a hill-walk sometime if it didn't take up so much time'. He then proceeded to amplify the statement by inferring that a whole day was wasted on such a pastime whereas something like a game of squash only took an hour. (He plays squash.) This short exchange, to my mind, seems to encapsulate the yawning gulf in communication and understanding between hillwalkers and non-hillwalkers, or more generally between mountaineers and non-mountaineers. As I persuasively tried to point out, his argument seemed only to imply that the reason we go hillwalking or play squash is to keep fit. If that were the case, we may as well spend an hour running up and down the stairs.

The brief discourse also sharply illustrated the thinking and ideals of an 'instant society'. People want quick solutions to everything, whether it be dieting, entertainment, meals, or keeping fit. Having mentioned meals, it is somewhat appropriate here to throw up a direct analogy – between a game of squash and an instant microwave meal, and a day's hillwalk and a seven-course dinner. The crucial point in all this is the enjoyment aspect. Of course there is enjoyment in playing squash, or jogging, or skiing, just as there is enjoyment in eating an instant meal, but the pleasure in all these things is effectively transient – it does not stand the test of time. The enjoyment gained by mountaineering breaks the bonds of the here and now and encourages long-term reflective gratification. I have climbed and skied for many years in Scotland and not one single day's skiing (of the downhill, piste-bashing variety) stands out as highly memorable – in fact very few stand out for any reason. In comparison, there are very few mountaineering days which *do not* stand out for one reason or another. Climbing Munros on skis, however, can be a most compelling and rewarding winter pastime, and the two facets of Nordic skiing and ski-mountaineering are both popular pursuits. The publication of the SMC guide *Ski Mountaineering in Scotland* in 1987 is a reflection of this growing popularity.

The question 'why climb?' or 'why go hillwalking?' customarily emanates from non-climbing friends, and the ensuing discussion inevitably develops into a quasi-philosophical dialogue seemingly at complete variance with the concrete reality of the mountain. Yet at the deepest level, the real reason why countless mountain-lovers return again and again to the hills is more than to enjoy themselves, have fun and keep fit – the experience also seems to nurture a more profound, almost spiritual awareness of themselves and their surroundings.

This chapter will attempt to address the question 'why climb Munros?', although the discussion will necessarily draw parallels with the reasons for engaging in other mountain activities, such as rock-climbing and scrambling. There no doubt exist those individuals who take the view that 'analysis equals paralysis' and that no amount of examination and dissection can explain the underlying motivation of the hill-going fraternity. Nevertheless, what follows will hopefully throw some light on this often-asked question.

Mountaineering in its broadest sense can be seen to involve three aspects of enjoyment in varying degrees of refinement and subtlety. The first is what could be termed the 'fun-and-fresh-air' aspect and is the most basic and clear-cut of the three. Then there is the 'adventure-and-challenge' aspect, which involves slightly more delicate and complex ideas. Finally, there is the 'mysticism-and-beauty' aspect, which is the most subtle and profound of the three. It should be said that the three aspects are not mutually exclusive, each interrelating with the others to build up a broad spectrum of enjoyable experiences. Each of these aspects will now be looked at in some detail, starting with 'fun and fresh air'.

Probably the main reason people piste ski is because it offers immediate thrills and fun in the open air with no need for any uphill

'Fun and fresh air':
Kilgraston school-
girls nearing the
summit of
Ben Lawers

trudges. Excitement and exhilaration are the name of the game. Does climbing a Munro really arouse the same sensation? Most people would answer no, simply because the fun aspect is more obvious in skiing, but it is also more transitory. Children or young adults are a fairly rare commodity walking on the hills of Britain, but the ski slopes are choking with them. The majority of youngsters live for the moment and enjoy the excitement of the here and now – hence skiing is ideal for them. Hillwalking, on the other hand, is a slow, grinding, reflective pastime which by its very nature is more appealing to the pensive, plodding older person. Of course, we mustn't over-generalise here: lots of adults (including me) enjoy skiing, just as plenty of children enjoy climbing Munros.

The 'fun' involved in hillwalking originates from countless little things: the wind on your face, the views, the joy of exploration, the companionship of others, reaching the top, spotting a herd of deer, the feeling of well-being – the list is endless. In the final analysis, a successful hill-walk or climb is ultimately more satisfying than a day's skiing because there is an objective in view – reaching the summit, or completing the route. Downhill skiing involves much time spent standing around in queues and considerably less on short, stimulating runs, but it is inevitably an aimless activity. At the end of a year the hillwalker can look back and ponder with satisfaction that he or she has climbed so many Munros; a definite, quantifiable result has been established. The skier, however, can only reflect on an endless series of almost identical descents, and perhaps that he can now perform a semi-respectable parallel turn!

A keen hillwalking pupil of mine once remarked that one of the reasons she enjoyed walking on a Sunday was that it set her up for the week, both mentally and physically. At the time, I thought that this was quite a sophisticated and adult observation, but absolutely true. The 'healthy body – healthy mind' notion may be rather clichéd but the feeling of well-being resulting from a long hill-walk is undeniable and often lasts for many days. A similar feeling can also result from other athletic pursuits but is rarely so intense or as long lasting.

For most hill-goers, the weather is a significant factor in the enjoyment of a day in the hills, for obvious reasons. Yet it is precisely the fickle variability of Britain's weather which helps produce the enormous range of experiences and emotions felt by the hillwalker. A typical day for a party of hillwalkers might begin in an atmosphere of serene peace, with the sun on their backs and a light cooling breeze on their faces. Later on, as the summit ridge is reached, the wind might have strengthened to almost hurricane proportions and frequent ferocious rainy squalls force them to don cagoules and woolly hats. Still later, the cloud level might drop to envelope them in a clammy cloak of mist and finding the cairn becomes a battle against the odds. Then on the descent the rain and clouds might clear (as is often the case) and the sun again brings new warmth and fervour to the land:

> *But soon after the rain*
> *The liquid sun spills*
> *Columns of light through curtains of mist*
> *And arouses leaden hills*
>
> *A million water beads*
> *Cling inert to grassy stems*
> *Now translucent, transmuted by the sun*
> *To myriad sparkling gems.*

Foul weather clothing is immediately cast off and a sparkling freshness seems to invigorate the very air they breathe.

Such is the range and diversity of weather conditions that can be encountered on a single day on the Scottish hills, which essentially contributes to the richness of the whole experience. Much later they might bask luxuriously in the warm glow of a cosy pub totally immersed in the conviviality and camaraderie of others who have perhaps shared their

A million water
beads cling inert to
grassy stems

experience. Such an end to the day is a marvellous contrast to the athletic
fray on the hill and inevitably leads to absolute consummated contentment.

On days when the weather has shown its ugly side for most or all of the
time, and the whole day has been an almost epic struggle for survival, the
contrast between the wild mountain and the warm pub becomes more
pronounced, as does the intense feeling of accomplishment and satisfaction.
This naturally leads on to the second aspect of enjoyment involved in
mountaineering – that of 'adventure and challenge'.

Perhaps the most common response from the mountaineer when asked
to explain his or her motivation to climb is the challenge. The mountaineer
has an overwhelming desire to explore unknown areas, to test himself on
new routes and new mountains and to generally satisfy a restless spirit
which thrives on the lure, mystery and danger of the unknown. The
'unknown' may be familiar to others but it is unknown to the newcomer, and
that is all that matters. The additional benefits of exploring and surviving
in literally unknown mountain domains are vast, and opportunities for such
pioneering are gradually diminishing as the human race spreads to all
corners of the globe.

Unfortunately, the days of original exploration in Britain are long since
past, in the sense that all the wilderness country has been mapped and all the
mountains climbed. Yet climbing mountains is one thing; climbing them by
different routes is another. In that sense there is still a vast amount of
unexplored, untouched territory. New rock-climbing and ice-climbing routes

are continually being 'discovered' and recorded, reaching ever more extreme standards of difficulty. In a sense, winter climbing routes are effectively infinite, as the formation of snow and ice changes from year to year.

Where does all this leave the poor old hillwalker who basically climbs mountains by the easiest well-trodden routes? To Himalayan 'tigers' who attempt unclimbed routes on the hardest faces of 8,000m peaks, the challenge of walking up the Ben Lomond tourist path on a sunny day is effectively minimal or non-existent. Yet the same could not be said of, say, Hugh Munro's epic struggle on the Cairngorm plateau in failing light in mid-winter (see Chapter 1), or of Martin Moran's avalanche experience on Ben Wyvis (Chapter 4). The crucial point here is that objective mountain danger is *always* a potential hazard, regardless of height, mountain, season or route. Even more crucially, 'challenge' is a very subjective word. To a relatively unfit, overweight novice who has never climbed a Munro, the Ben Lomond tourist path assumes the status of their own personal Everest. Each individual's concept of challenge is unique to them – whether it be the Eiger north face in winter, the Cuillin Ridge in a day, or the traverse of Aonach Eagach. The beauty of the mountains, including the Munros, is that they can be anything to anyone.

Those taking their first faltering steps into the hills are usually accompanied by more experienced friends and tackle fairly easy summer

'Adventure and challenge': a misty day on the Mamore Ridge

routes such as Ben Lomond, Beinn Ime or Schiehallion. Gradually, as more confidence and experience is gained, longer ridges and whole groups of Munros are climbed, such as Ben Cruachan and the Five Sisters of Kintail. Also at this stage, an ice-axe and crampons may have been purchased in order to experience the greater challenge and more acute joys of winter hillwalking. Still later, the craggier pinnacled delights of Aonach Eagach, Liathach, An Teallach and ultimately the Cuillin Ridge of Skye will begin to beckon, as the joys of scrambling become more pronounced. Some may venture further still and tackle routes like Curved Ridge on Buachaille Etive Mor or Tower Ridge on Ben Nevis, and then attempt the same routes in winter. Also at this stage, or before, many will have developed the experience and confidence to indulge in solo ventures, with all the extra care and awareness that these demand. Others will discover peace and contentment in long backpacking trips through wilderness areas like Knoydart and the Fisherfield forest, collecting various Munros *en route*. The simple pleasures of wild camping and bothying become part of the whole experience and possibly ends in themselves. For those whose thirst for adventure and challenge has still not been fully quenched, a vast store of potential adventure yet remains: wilderness camping in winter, snowholing, ice-climbing, ski-mountaineering, cross-country skiing, extreme skiing, extreme rock-climbing, fell-running . . . the list is endless.

The challenge inherent in all these ventures, from a summer ascent of Ben Lomond to a solo ascent of Zero Gully on Ben Nevis, totally depends on the experience of the individual. The important point to realise is that as experience increases, so too will the amount of objective danger with which the individual will be willing to flirt. Many accidents on the hills today are caused by individuals not having the experience to realise how much objective danger they *are* able to cope with. In other words, they are attempting routes which at the time are beyond their own limitations.

Although the challenge involved in climbing Munros can be compared with that involved in other mountain pursuits, such as rock-climbing, their attraction lies in their relative accessibility to a large proportion of the population. (In the sense that rock-climbing requires suitable preliminary training.) In other words, anyone who is relatively fit and can put one foot in front of another is potentially able to begin climbing Munros. Secondly, the challenge they present is both individual and comprehensive. Individual in the sense of each separate Munro offering its own unique challenge depending on route, season, weather, etc., and comprehensive in the sense that the 277 Munros offer a global challenge taken as a whole. It is this comprehensive challenge which probably more than anything else motivates the dedicated Munro-bagger to continue his quest.

It is interesting to imagine a scenario where no list of 3,000-foot peaks in Scotland existed and the word 'Munro' was just somebody's surname. Would there still be similar numbers of hillwalkers flocking to the hills? It is extremely doubtful. Most people like having a framework or scheme to work to, and the Munros provide this perfectly. They bring a methodology and motivation to what some may see as an essentially aimless activity – wandering the hills. Without the long-term objective of completing the Munros, many hillwalkers would lack the almost obsessive drive and motivation which takes them out again and again in all weathers. The sense of freedom, fun, fresh-air, the appreciation of the beauty of the mountain world and the increased awareness of one's surroundings are all additional contributory motivational factors which must be present to a greater or lesser extent, otherwise the whole exercise becomes a pointless charade.

A.E. Robertson, the first Munroist, in his early article 'The Munros of Scotland', recalls a conversation in which he described to a friend his experiences in climbing every hill over 3,000 feet in Scotland. His friend did not see the point of this at all and flippantly commented, 'Why would you want to climb every hill? No one has ever kissed every lamp-post in Princes Street, and why should anyone want to?' Robertson then proceeds to make the point that he had never looked at the matter in this 'profane light', which partly illustrates the notion that few mountaineers ever ask why they climb mountains, or conversely that it is usually non-mountaineers who ask the question. Kissing the cairns of Munros and kissing all the lamp-posts in Princes Street are indeed comparable occupations, but only to unimaginative, unadventurous, spiritless individuals.

So much for the challenge of the Munros. What about adventure? Challenge and adventure almost go hand in hand, but not quite. Every adventure by its very nature must carry a risk factor and therefore involve a challenge, but not every challenging enterprise is necessarily adventurous. Kissing all the lamp-posts in Edinburgh would certainly constitute a monumental challenge but could in no way be described as adventurous. Zany, eccentric and deranged, yes; adventurous, no! An adventure is a potentially hazardous enterprise, usually in wild country, far removed from the petty frustrations of a pampered, centrally heated urban existence. It is essentially because of this cosseted, mechanised lifestyle that these frustrations build up and we feel an overpowering desire to escape to the hills and immerse our souls in the solitude and serenity which only they can offer.

Recreational mountaineering was almost unheard of not so very long ago when less automation and less holidays made earning a living a full-time occupation. Now the opportunities for mountaineering and other recreational pursuits are limitless, yet more and more people are underexercised. The 'instant-society' notion mentioned at the beginning of this chapter requires people to be entertained by TV, video, computer games, etc., with little or no input from the individual. In short, it encourages laziness, lethargy and vegetation. Stress and frustration inevitably arise from this inert existence. In extreme cases, some people resort to mindless vandalism and violence to find a release. Some others, more positively, take to the hills. An increasing number of people are discovering that the simulated pseudo-adventures found on TV and films do not satisfy a craving for real challenge and adventure, and that climbing Munros does.

We now turn to the third and most esoteric facet of enjoyment in mountaineering, the 'mysticism-and-beauty' aspect. Generally speaking, this particular aspect only emerges with maturity and experience and is the most complex and abstract to explain to the non-mountaineer. Once it has flourished and ripened within the innermost self it underpins the very foundation of our enjoyment of the hills and profoundly underlies our passion and the wish to continue climbing. The 'beauty' aspect of mountains will be explored first, and this leads on naturally to the mystical, spiritual aspect.

Mountains, or mountainous landscapes, are often described using superlatives such as majestic, awesome, grand, sublime, savage, elemental or wild. All these adjectives conjure up the image of a barren vastness which many people, particularly in pre-Victorian times, would consider to be anything but beautiful. It is only in the last century that preconceptions and prejudices have been removed and people have gradually been conditioned into seeing mountains as beautiful.

Everyone is familiar with the stereotypical picture-postcard or calendar view of a placid Highland scene complete with blue sky and loch, snow-capped peaks and sunshine. Most people, even some non-mountain-lovers, appreciate to a greater or lesser extent the beauty in such a scene. However, perhaps only a few hours after the photographer took the shot, bad weather may have closed in and obscured the mountain in a driving barrage of sleet, wind and mist. Where is the beauty now? Yet many or all of the superlatives listed above in describing the beauty of mountain landscape perfectly encapsulate this new scenario, particularly savage, elemental and wild. It is almost as if mountain beauty has a dual personality; a kind of Jekyll and Hyde dichotomy which is essential to its very existence. 'The reality' of mountain beauty derives from both the serene and the savage.

Awesome and ruthless upheavals produced the serenity of the mountains we see today. The cataclysmic forces of the last ice age together with extremes of pressure and temperature produced the corries, arêtes and graceful ridges. On a more day-to-day basis it is the driving rain and melting

Winter in the
Scottish Highlands:
a view from the
summit of
Ben Chonzie in
Perthshire

Winter evening sun
on the summit
ridge of Buachaille
Etive Mor

Winter at its best: temperature inversion on the Tarmachan Ridge

OPPOSITE TOP: Beinn Dearg Mor, a rugged and remote Corbett in the north-western Highlands. Shenavall Bothy is in the foreground

OPPOSITE BOTTOM: The far north-west: the view from the Corbett of Cul Mor looking towards Stac Polly (a Graham)

A Graham from a Corbett: the Pap of Glencoe from Garbh Bheinn, Loch Leven

A Munro from a Graham: Bla Bheinn from Marsco, Skye (see Chapter 9)

The glorious view
from Beinn na
h-Eaglaise
(a Torridonian
Graham) looking
towards the Corbett
of Sgurr Dubh.
Mighty Liathach
and Beinn Eighe
form the left-hand
skyline

The fragility of
nature
(see Chapter 10)

The original
woodland: a small
remnant of
Caledonian pines in
Coire Mhic Nobuil,
Torridon. The
Horns of Alligin are
visible beyond
(see Chapter 10)

Proud the lonely
rowan stands: the
Blackmount from
Rannoch Moor

Leaving the summit
of Ben Lawers at
the end of a
spectacular winter's
day. Ben More and
Stob Binnein are on
the horizon

snow which produce the peaceful tranquillity of rivers and lochs, the vibrancy of colour and the lushness of vegetation. It is the wind-driven sleet and snow which are ultimately responsible for the formation of elegantly furled cornices, wind-blasted furrows and fragile ice sculptures. Even the light which enables us to see this beauty has its source at the fiery, tempestuous heart of the sun. Beauty and the Beast walk hand in hand. Without the Beast there would be no Beauty.

In Scotland it could be said that we have more than our fair share of the Beast but, as the above examples illustrates, this implies that we also have more than our fair share of Beauty. How true! Scotland has often been described as the most scenically beautiful small country in the world, and this is no exaggeration. It is precisely the variability and extremes of Scottish weather which help create the staggeringly subtle and moody landscapes which are the hallmarks of Highland beauty.

Yet there is an elusive, almost intangible nature to this beauty. Somehow, the most exquisite mountain views are exceptionally transient. The constantly shifting clouds and light patterns, the soft pastel shades, the infinitely varied gold and russet tones of autumn, the delicate mist on distant ridges, the freshness after a storm; all these, and more, in various combinations give Scottish mountains a dynamic vibrance which is lacking in the world's greater ranges such as the Alps or Himalaya.

Experiencing this beauty involves more than just seeing with the eyes: it has to be seen with the heart, it has to be felt, it has to entail an active interaction between the landscape and the very soul of the observer, or rather participator. Without this interaction the beauty collapses to that of a calendar image, superficial and skin deep. Only by physically entering into the heart of the mountain domain can we come to a closer recognition and understanding of its allure. It is precisely the effort and hardship which mountaineers endure in pursuit of their goal that produces the potential for experiencing this mystical communion between man and mountain. Aesthetic appreciation which is borne out of toil is infinitely more profound, intense and long lasting than that acquired from brief flickering glimpses from a car or coach window. If, in addition to toil, there is also an element of danger involved, feelings of rapturous euphoria can result on completion of a particularly hazardous section of the climb. This, in turn, enhances the responsiveness of the mind to the surrounding beauty.

It is the intense and enduring quality of the mountaineer's appreciation of his environment that calls him or her back to the hills again and again. Over the years, a wealth of experiences are accumulated, whether it be through climbing Munros or through rock- or ice-climbing, and yields a truer understanding of the mystical nature of mountains. Notice, 'a truer understanding' and not 'a true understanding'. Capturing the ultimate mystery of the mountains is akin to catching an elusive butterfly – just when it appears to be trapped it flutters off into the blue. It is an eternal quest, like taking the finest photograph, writing the greatest poem, painting the greatest picture: there is always something better, always room for improvement. That is the ultimate reason for returning to the hills, to become closer to the elusive goal.

It is often claimed that mountaineering is a form of escapism. Hill-goers themselves talk of escaping to the hills for a day or for a weekend. Non-mountaineers would normally interpret escapism as escape from reality, escape from the 'real world' of cities, cars, offices and computers. That is indeed what the mountaineer is escaping from, but his definition of reality is not the artificial, automated world of modern man, but the natural, uncluttered world of the mountains. In other words, the climber is not escaping *from* reality but escaping *to* reality. Deep in the heart of the hills, the mountaineer is completely free of the ignominious face of contemporary society with all its false morals and vanity. Indeed, he has found peace, contentment and a total absence of frustration and confusion. The stresses and strains of modern living can never be totally abandoned, but the mountains provide a calm haven and refuge in which to view petty frustrations in a truer perspective.

On some of the more popular Munros, and especially at weekends, the aforementioned peace and contentment may be difficult to find, and in these situations the hillwalker may well resort to seeking out alternative routes or exploring some of the more inaccessible peaks.

Perhaps the ultimate in escapism is the somewhat controversial pursuit of solitary mountaineering. Frowned upon by the Philistines but adored by the devout, the activity has always been popular and, for many, preferable to 'going with the crowd'. It is not the intention here to explore in detail the rights and wrongs of solo mountaineering, but rather to examine the reasons for its wide acclaim among a good proportion of the hill-going fraternity.

'Never go alone' is one of the oft-remembered 'rules' of hillwalking, and certainly for the novice hillwalker no sounder advice could be given. However, for those with a solid foundation of experience and the confidence and craving to indulge in a solo hill-walk, there can be fewer more enlightening experiences. The absence of companions is comparable to the severing of the 'umbilical cord' connecting us to the rest of humanity. We are no longer dependent on others or they on us. We become absolutely dependent on ourselves. Arising from this independence from human relationships emerges a greater, more accurate awareness of beauty, of the spiritual nature of the mountains and of ourselves.

In my own particular case, over half my Munro ascents have been solitary excursions, but more to the point these are the ones which generally stand out as being the most memorable. Why should this be? Hillwalking companions to a large extent are a diversion which effectively devaluate and diminish the total mountain experience. Without them, this experience impinges on the memory with an overwhelming poignancy. This may seem quite a selfish and egotistical remark to make, but most hillwalkers would agree that ascending Ben Nevis by the tourist path with a jostling crowd of chattering individuals bears little resemblance to a solo ascent of Ledge Route, a scrambling route on the north face of the same mountain. This extreme example serves to illustrate that large groups of people on the hills at any one time are not conducive to the individual's private communion with the mountain landscape. Even one or two companions detract from this intimate interaction. Of course, there are occasions when we do not wish to be completely alone and feel the desire to share our experiences with others, especially those who are new to the game. Often, the eagerness and enthusiasm of the novice is highly infectious and can be a boost to the possibly flagging spirits of other members of the party. In short, solo hillwalking has its unique place but never to the total exclusion of walking with companions.

The merits of solitary hillwalking are somewhat akin to those of winter hillwalking. The greater alertness required when the days are shorter and snow and ice are underfoot nurtures a more acute awareness of the surroundings. Scotland's mountains under a blanket of snow possess an austere but awesome beauty and present the climber with a greater depth of experience and challenge than in summer conditions. Much has already been made in previous chapters of the virtues of winter mountaineering, and those fortunate individuals who have experienced the reassuring squeak of crampons on hard névé while traversing a sunlit snow ridge or watched distant, icy spires become slowly flushed fiery salmon pink with the setting sun will understand completely the charismatic spell of the winter mountain domain. Perhaps the most profoundly uplifting mountain experience is to combine the solo and winter aspects and undertake a solitary winter hillwalk. Obviously, the level of experience required to indulge in such a committed venture should be substantial and backed up by a good number of winter hillwalks with company.

This chapter began by drawing a comparison between hillwalking and playing squash. Similarly, a comparison can be made between any branch of mountaineering and organised competitive sport in general. It is hoped that this chapter has gone some way in conveying the notion that mountain-eering is more than just mere sport, more than just a contest between two teams or individuals. In this sense, mountaineering is, of course, the very antithesis of competitive games. In hillwalking or climbing there are no competitors other than the mountains themselves, and yet we never really 'conquer' a mountain, only flirt with its potential dangers. Reaching the summit may be important, but it is only one incident in a physical and spiritual journey whose ultimate aim is to acquire through exploration a deeper understanding and appreciation of mountain beauty in all weathers and seasons.

For the peak-bagger it is perhaps all too easy to become partially blind to this beauty and rate the success of a day only in terms of the number of Munros climbed. Here, the exploratory urge is being stifled and the real mountain experience is being reduced to a record-breaking, goal-scoring competitiveness which may eventually cloud the vision which attracted the individual to the hills in the first instance.

There exists a growing number of hill-goers who are totally dismissive of the whole Munro-bagging mentality, arguing that the peak-collecting syndrome produces people who are unaware of mountain landscapes and moods and only interested in the summit cairn. Perhaps the best known of these is Jim Crumley, one of the finest exponents of the spiritual beauty of Scotland's wild landscapes. His deep observations are contained in the excellent *A High and Lonely Place* (a book about the Cairngorms) and, more recently, *Among Mountains*. His reasons for climbing mountains are clear on the one hand – 'I go among mountains to be among mountains' – but also decidedly enigmatic and ethereal to those whose interests lie in other areas.

The stance adopted by Jim Crumley regarding the 'climb-every-Munro-brigade' is an extreme one. The majority of hillwalkers, I believe, are not peak-bagging automatons, unreceptive to the finer aspects of the mountain environment, but are physically (and often spiritually) aware of a deeper reality. Too many Munro-baggers *are* dressed in 'head-to-toe, state-of-the-art technicolours', but that is more the fault of the manufacturers of mountain equipment than the consumer of such garish garments – try getting hold of a moss-green fleece jacket nowadays!

Jim makes the comment, 'You can tell a weekend Munro from a great distance by the fact that it is awash with people being seen and not seeing, being heard and not hearing.' Certainly, in summer the summit cairns of many popular Munros such as Ben Lomond and Ben Lawers are indeed awash with multi-coloured chattering individuals, but who has the right to deny them taking pleasure in Scottish hills in this way? The 'fun-and-fresh-air' aspect (mentioned earlier) may rise to the fore, and usually does, when large groups of people take to climbing one mountain, and the spiritual side may well be fleeting or totally absent. But surely this is all part of the total mountain experience? I have already made my own position clear on solitary hill-walking, but walking with companions has its own pleasures which cannot be denied.

Jim Crumley's hatred of Munro-bagging is distilled in the remark that it (Munro-bagging) 'denies the greatest of all mountain joys – the joy of being there'. Personally, I find this statement hard to swallow. Surely it is the joy of being there that takes us all back to the hills again and again, regardless of whether we have climbed a Munro, Corbett, Graham or visited a high hill loch? True, in many cases reaching the summit cairn becomes the driving preoccupation but never totally to the exclusion of just 'being there'. There is a story about two lone hillwalkers who passed each other on the ridge between Gleouraich and Spidian Mialach. Each shouted to the other a single number (the number of the Munros they had climbed) and continued on their separate ways with nothing else being said. No doubt they both returned to their lonely one-man tents and derived great pleasure and satisfaction from adding two more ticks to their respective copies of Munro's Tables! It is undoubtedly this mentality which Jim finds repugnant, and when list-ticking *is* the overriding factor above all else then he is absolutely right.

The joy of list-ticking and the joy of being there are not two mutually exclusive pleasures but are, I believe, both powerful complementary facets which are present in most hillwalkers to a greater or lesser extent. As Hamish Brown remarks, the list-ticking aspect 'brings a drive and discipline to wandering feet'; Munro-bagging has introduced the pleasures of the hills to vast numbers and has also provided a great challenge, which simply aimless wandering and 'being there' on their own cannot supply. Like Everest, the Munros are there. Why not try to climb them all?

In the final analysis, it should be quality and not quantity which is the criterion of a successful day on the hills. On the most superficial level, a successful hill day is appraised only on its Munro count. On a deeper level, it is remembered fondly for the rustle of wind in the trees, the chatter of grouse on the moor, perhaps the first cuckoo, the haunting roar of a distant rutting stag, bog cotton tossing gently in the breeze, the smell of bog-myrtle and pine, and countless other subtle sights, sounds and smells.

At the deepest level, it is a reflective, but profoundly intense spiritual communion with the whole mountain landscape, from the moss and heather under our feet to the furthest ridge crest. The mountains form the chief ingredient of this communion; they provide the roughage for the spiritual nourishment so essential to a truer understanding of them and ultimately ourselves.

CHAPTER 9

Beyond the Munros

The grandeur, grace, or technical problems of a hill do not necessarily increase with height, nor does it follow the character or interest of the ridges are enhanced, or a view improved, the higher we go. In fact, and this is the point I seek to make for my Lists, it is only since I began visiting these lower hills have I seen, appreciated, and enjoyed the full majesty of the mightier ones in Munro's Tables to which classification Scotland's hillwalkers like me owe so much.

William M. Docharty

Is there life after the Munros? Have all the thousand-plus 'compleaters' hung up their well-worn boots and sunk into an armchair by the fireside to reminisce fondly over scores of happy hill days? As I said at the end of Chapter 6, nothing could be further from the truth: 'Completing the Munros is not the end, it is only the beginning.' This chapter aims to explain in some detail just what many Munroists do once the search for their holy grail is over.

It should be clearly evident from the last chapter that the many years of experience gained in climbing Munros should awaken and kindle a growing flame of passionate affection for the Scottish hills in all their moods. It is almost unthinkable that this fiery passion should suddenly become unquenched on completion of the Munros. Mixed feelings of euphoria and sadness are bound to affect the Munroist for a short spell after completion, but the intensity of feeling for the mountains will eventually spur him on to fresh challenges.

In my own particular case, several short challenges presented themselves and one extensive longer challenge – the Corbetts. As I briefly mentioned in Chapter 6 the short challenges consisted of compiling and completing a list of classic scrambling routes in Scotland, and also a long-distance walk from Kintyre to Cape Wrath. This will be discussed in more detail later on.

It is probably true, though certainly unproven, that the bulk of 'compleaters' go on to work their way through other lists of hills such as

Tops, Corbetts, Furth of Scotland and other more obscure collections such as Donalds, Wainwrights, Bridges, Grahams and Marilyns! All will be revealed in this chapter. For the moment we shall begin with the least-inspired class of Munroists: those who climb all the Munros again. Perhaps this is a slightly disparaging label as a good proportion of the 50 or so 'secondary Munroists' have no doubt completed their second rounds in conjunction with attempts on the other lists described above. One of the reasons why Munro-bagging has achieved such cult status (though obviously not the main one) is that Munro's Tables contain a list of Munroists within its covers. People love to see their name in print, and this is another incentive to complete the round. There is also the additional satisfaction of purchasing a tie, complete with the Munro crest from Chris Huntley,* the Clerk of the List. No such incentive exists for any of the other lists, although those completing the Tops and Furth are listed in earlier editions of Munro's Tables, and they are, in fact, still listed in the *SMC Journal*. Munro's Tables continually updates its list of Munroists in new editions (giving name and year of completion) and also years of further completions for secondary and 'poly-Munroists'.

The question of why some people embark on a second round is not as difficult to answer as it may seem initially. After all, if they enjoyed climbing them the first time why shouldn't they enjoy climbing them again? The immediate reaction to this would probably be that they do not present the same challenge second time round. If climbed by the same route, in the same season with the same weather then this reaction has some substance. Buachaille Etive Mor by the normal walker's route on a typically wet Scottish summer day is a world away from the same mountain by the scrambling route of Curved Ridge on a cloudless winter day in January. A deliberate policy of some Munroists on their second round is to reverse the season and change the route on each Munro or group of Munros. For instance, an ascent of the Ben Lawers range in summer from the visitor centre can be updated next time round to a winter circuit beginning in Glen Lyon, which incidentally is an altogether more natural and satisfying route. By consciously searching out less-frequented, non-guide-book routes, the hillwalker is continually fostering the exploratory spirit. The Munros have a lot more to offer than their normal routes of ascent.

An interesting idea from one particular Munroist is to climb each Munro by an exceptionally classic route, or in some cases by *the* classic route. For instance, Ben Nevis by Tower Ridge, Ben Lui by Central Gully, Sgurr nan Gillean by Pinnacle Ridge or the Saddle by the Forcan Ridge. At first sight, this idea seems a good one, but unfortunately we soon run into

* Old Medwyn, Spittal, Carnwath, Lanarkshire ML11 8LY.

trouble on Munros such as Meall Buidhe, Meall Ghaordie, Meall Chuaich and dozens of other up-turned pudding bowls, which have about as many classic routes as a slag heap in Sunderland. Perhaps, in cases like these, rather than try to contrive a 'classic' *route* it is more productive to devise an interesting or even unusual means of ascending or traversing the hill, by, for example, the use of skis, mountain-bike or even paraglider. As far as I know, no one has yet made a paragliding descent from every Munro – another crazy challenge awaits any takers.

Another obvious, though time-consuming challenge is to undertake a continuous round of the Munros in a single expedition. First realised by Hamish Brown in 1974 and subsequently by a handful of others, a continual Munro traverse will appeal to those who love to become totally immersed in the Scottish hills for long periods of time. A relatively unhurried round will take three months at the minimum, and it is evident that very few people will have the time, and indeed inclination, to indulge in a lengthy venture requiring such commitment. More will be said about long-distance backpacking trips later in this chapter, but for the moment we turn to what is undoubtedly the most common post-Munro activity, that of working through other lists of mountains such as Tops and Corbetts.

There are 517 distinct summits over 3,000 feet in Scotland, of which 277 receive full mountain status, and are known as the Munros. The remaining 240 summits constitute the Tops, which seem the obvious target to go for once the Munros are finished. Up until the Sixties over half of the tally of Munroists had also completed the Tops. Since then the proportion has dwindled significantly and now only about one in ten has 'Topped up'. Today it is fairly rare to find someone climbing Munros and Tops simultaneously. Possibly because more people now are content with minimum standards, Tops seem to have gone quietly 'out of fashion'. This may seem oddly surprising considering that they are in effect secondary Munros and just as eligible and worthy as their parent summits. With the emergence of such guide-books as *The Munros* and *The Munro Almanac*, it is perhaps understandable that the hillwalker is going to concentrate on bagging Munros since these alone are listed.

The joy of exploration is a highly influential factor in the motivation of the hillwalker. By their very nature the Tops are linked to the main Munro summits by connecting ridges and therefore fail to take the hillwalker into completely new mountain areas. The exploratory pleasure of climbing Tops, particularly after completing the Munros, is accordingly much less than that gained in, say, tackling the 3,000-footers Furth of Scotland or the Corbetts. One weakness of the Furth of Scotland peaks is their diverse yet locally clustered geographical locations in the Lake District and Wales, although the Irish 3,000-footers are well scattered. The

Ben Vrackie, a fine and popular Corbett, rising high above Pitlochry

beauty of the Munros is their more-or-less random distribution throughout the Highlands of Scotland, and also their great number. On a rough Munro basis, Furth of Scotland comprises less than 20 3,000-foot mountains – not exactly a long-term challenge.

None of these drawbacks apply to the Corbetts. Despite those who condemn the Corbetts as being 'old men's Munros', in many respects they provide a greater challenge and take the walker far further afield than their more popular big brothers. John Rooke Corbett, who originated the list of 2,500-foot mountains in Scotland, was briefly mentioned at the beginning of Chapter 3 and we now give a more detailed profile of the man and his list.

J.R. Corbett was an Englishman based in Bristol and a district valuer by trade. An enthusiastic member of the Scottish Mountaineering Club, he served on the committee and also became the fourth Munroist and the second person to climb the Munros *and* Tops in 1930. Corbett was a quiet, reserved man and an outstanding student at Cambridge University, where he developed a passion for long-distance walking – he once walked the 155 miles from Cambridge to his early home of Manchester. This interest in walking subsequently led to his becoming one of the original members of the Rucksack Club and eventually to his remarkable feat of climbing every hill in Scotland over 2,000 feet – over 700 hills. This phenomenonal achievement (even today) was finally completed in 1943, and shortly after this he suffered a heart attack which cut short his activities for a while. He did, however, restart walking, only to be further handicapped by a spreading paralytic affliction, and he died shortly after the war, aged 72. None of this does much to extol the health benefits of frequent walking.

Corbett's list of 2,500-foot summits was not published in his own lifetime. After his death his sister passed the list to the SMC, who subsequently included it in Munro's Tables with a few minor amendments. There was no written suggestion in Corbett's notes as to the rule he used in listing the hills included, but detailed analysis of the list implies almost conclusively that each hill had to have a re-ascent of 500 feet on all sides with no account taken of either distance or steepness. This stringent condition was rigorously applied to each peak listed.

The present list of Corbetts tallies at 221, but it should be pointed out that were it not for the strict 500-feet-of-re-ascent rule the total would be a great deal more – more than the number of Munros, in fact. Corbett himself provided no additional list of 'Corbett Tops', that is subsidiary 2,500-foot summits not classified as true Corbetts. The re-ascent rule ensures that Corbetts are well-defined and fairly detached summits, in contrast to the Munros, where there is no obvious criterion for deciding on separate Munros, and certainly nothing involving height drop between peaks. A striking example is that of the South Cluanie Ridge in Glen Shiel, which contains seven Munros in as many miles with the ridge dropping below 800m on only one occasion. More to the point, the height drop between successive Munros is rarely more than 140m, and an analysis of the ridge using a Corbett methodology would only produce three Corbetts at the most. Those budding peak-baggers expecting long ridges of easy Corbetts must therefore prepare to be disappointed. By their very nature, Corbetts rarely form themselves into self-contained and manageable groups, one of the few exceptions to this being the three Corbetts forming the high points of the summit ridge of Quinag in the north of Scotland.

There can be few, if any, Munroists, however single minded, who have not at some time in their Munro-bagging spree climbed the odd Corbett. How many hillwalkers go to Arran without climbing Goatfell? Can there really be anyone who has climbed all the Arrochar Alps except the Cobbler? How many Munroists complete their quest having never ascended such northerly delights as Cul Beag, Cul Mor, Quinag, Foinaven or Ben Loyal? Not to mention such famous non-Corbetts as Stac Polly and Suilven. It has been said that the complete Munroist knows the Highlands far more deeply and intimately than any car-bound tourist. This is undoubtedly the case, but it is even more true for one who has also completed the Corbetts. The Corbetts are more than the foothills and outliers of Munros. This is, however, only part of the story. It is true that in the bulk of the Southern and Central Highlands many Corbetts are grossly overshadowed by their more popular Munro neighbours, but who could fail to be smitten by the individual charms of peaks like the Cobbler, Ben Vrackie, Ben Ledi and the Fara? The Corbetts true appeal is evident where they personify the very character of an area, and indeed form the principal peaks. The wilderness area of Ardgour and Moidart to the west of Loch Linnhe, for instance, contains no Munros, but the fine rocky peaks of Garbh Bheinn, Sgurr Ghiubsachain and Rois-Bheinn (to name a few) epitomise totally this unique landscape and are among the finest mountains in the whole of Scotland. Similarly, in the far north-west beyond Ullapool, where Munros are thin on the ground, Corbetts and other small peaks dominate the rough lochan-studded moorland in the shape of grand, isolated sandstone stumps.

The islands of Arran, Jura, Rum and Harris all boast Corbetts but no Munros and these, together with scores of small hills, characterise the unique sea-bound mountain domains so distinctive of these offshore havens. It is easy for the Munro-bagger to become blinkered by the Black Cuillin of Skye, and although the island possesses only two Corbetts it has a wealth of other smaller hills and ridges providing excellent scope for easy or challenging hill walks.

As well as new areas of the Highlands and Islands, the ascent of the Corbetts also brings the walker to southern Scotland and the Borders. Hills such as the Merrick and Broad Law again dominate the wild, rolling landscapes of Galloway and the Border country.

Even in areas of western Scotland seemingly eclipsed by the more widely known charms of Munros, such as Knoydart and Torridon, Corbetts full of character abound, such as Ben Aden, Sgurr Coire Choinnichean, Beinn Damh and Baosbheinn.

Without a doubt, the pursuit of Corbetts is a worthy and commendable post-Munro challenge, and hopefully what has already been said will have reinforced this notion. Many hillwalkers, and Hamish Brown in particular, advocate the simultaneous ticking off of Munros and Corbetts, although it is doubtful if many actually do this – even Hamish! The Munros present a nice tidy list to be completed, as do the Corbetts. Together they constitute a formidable mega-list of 498 peaks over 2,500 feet which, when tackled as a whole, form a daunting prospect.

The obvious allure and increasing popularity of Corbetts has increased in recent years with the publication of Hamish Brown's *Climbing the Corbetts* (Gollancz, 1988) and the Scottish Mountaineering Club's hillwalkers' guide volume two – *The Corbetts and Other Scottish Hills* (1990) (volume one being, of course, *The Munros*).

The Corbetts, Furth of Scotland and to some extent the Munro Tops provide the likeliest post-Munro challenge; but what lies beyond this? Restricting ourselves to Scotland for the moment, we find that Munro's Tables contain a third list of elevations – the Donalds. Compiled by Percy Donald, the list contains 138 Tops and hills in the Scottish *Lowlands* which are 2,000 feet or over. Eighty-seven of these elevations are defined to be true 'Hills' according to an arbitrary and frankly rather odd rule based on twelfth-of-a-mile units which will not be discussed here. Donald's list essentially covers all the main hills in the Ochils, the Borders, the Galloway hills and the Cheviots, with a few of the latter belonging to England.

The burning question, of course, is why did Donald restrict his list to the Scottish lowlands? It would appear that Donald, not being a Munroist, did not have the necessary knowledge, time or inclination to widen the scope to the Highlands, and besides, the task of climbing them all would be monumental. In recent years a can of worms has been opened regarding the classification and listing of the 2,000-foot peaks of Scotland, and what follows is an attempt to set the record straight.

A glance at the list of Munroists shows the thirteenth Munroist to be a man called William M. Docharty, who completed the Munros and Tops in 1948 and Furth of Scotland in 1949. Quite an unusual feat for the time, but more so considering that until late 1933 Docharty had stood on no Scottish hill apart from Ben Lomond in 1916 while on army leave. Not only that, but in 1918 he came within an ace of losing a leg while on active service.

On numerous occasions Docharty visited the Alps, delighting in their 'crystal atmosphere and virgin snow', but it was not until the autumn of 1933 that he first met John Thomson, who awakened in him an enthusiasm for the Scottish hills. A year before his completion of the Munros he became aware of a choice between two contrasting alternatives: 'To devote myself to a second series of excursions, with the Munros and their 3,000-foot subsidiaries once more as the principal objectives, or to open up a new series on fresh ground with these no more than incidental.'

Although he spent a week or so in the autumn of 1948 climbing the 3,000-foot hills of England, Wales and Ireland, two post-Munro excursions to Rum and Knoydart had 'left a profound impression upon me as to the latent possibilities of excursions on hills of sub-Munro standard'. By May of the following year he had decided to follow the second course of action, and conceived the idea of producing detailed lists of British mountains under 3,000 feet.

After several years of intensive peak-bagging, 1954 saw the publication of *A Selection of Some 900 British and Irish Mountain Tops*. This volume

William McKnight Docharty, who spent 14 years of his life climbing and classifying British mountains

contains a complete list of independent British and Irish mountains between 2,500 and 3,000 feet *and* subsidiary summits within this height range. Also included are some mountains of interest under 2,500 feet. One unique feature of the book is the inclusion of a series of superb panoramic black-and-white photographs, each constructed from several component prints, and of remarkable quality and clarity.

Although Docharty's primary criterion for independent mountain status was identical to Corbett's, i.e. a drop of 500 feet all round, the two lists differ in several respects. The obvious difference is that Docharty's list extends beyond Scotland, but in England he forsook the 500-foot rule for a 250-foot one, arguing that it excluded many individualistic summits. Also in Scotland, the 500-foot rule was relaxed in the Monadh Liath, Gaick Forest, Atholl and Glen Almond Tablelands as too many Tops were irrationally remote from their parent summits. (The criterion for a Top was only a 50-foot drop.) Docharty also saw fit to include borderline cases and points of interest on long, continuous ridges rising to over 3,000 feet. His classification of 2,500-foot Tops does not include 2,500-foot Tops of Munros but only of 2,500-foot separate mountains.

The first reaction to all this is probably a realisation of the complications and subjectivity which arise when attempting to classify mountains. Although Docharty's list goes far beyond Corbett's, its detailed complexity is probably the main reason for its exclusion from Munro's Tables. Out of 933 summits listed in Docharty's volume, 293 of them are classified as independent Scottish mountains between 2,500 and 3,000 feet. Corbett's far stricter application of the 500-foot rule, on the other hand, produced only 221 entries.

Docharty did not stop at 2,500 feet, however, and during the next eight years following the publication of his first volume he went on to climb and classify all the 2,000-foot summits (using the same criterion). Docharty was truly a man gripped by a magnificent obsession and in 1962 his second volume was published, bringing the grand total of mountains listed to 2,801, including many *under* 2000 feet. The monumental effort of such a self-imposed task is brushed aside by Docharty as 14 years of intense pleasure, 'to share with friends who have given me of their comradeship on lofty ridge and high plateau'. During those years, in Scotland alone Docharty recorded 541 excursions covering nearly 8,000 miles on foot or bike and climbing 1,628 different mountain tops.

But there is much more than mere statistics to this labour of love and a labour of love it certainly was. His two volumes not only contain lists of hills but also beautifully crafted prose which instantly tugs the heartstrings of all mountain-lovers. For instance, who could fail to be moved by this passage from his first volume:

And if I may leave a good wish with you on behalf of our Scottish hills, I should like it to be a crisp north-west breeze in your face before which the mists are reeling to disclose the vast blue firmament, in which not far above your head sail scattered squadrons of lofty snow-white spinnakers of fleecy cumulus, whose dark shadows stride swiftly athwart the course you have set on the ridges; around and beyond on other slopes and on the foothills below the speed of the shadows perceptively slackens – perhaps even they notice the gradient; while in yonder distances – offspring of the north-west wind – they are anchored like single islands or archipelagos on a placid tropical sea of palest powder blue.

Docharty also produced a third volume, or Epilogue, which is devoted entirely to his experiences (British and Alpine), and which also contains further marvellous panoramas. These photographs are a glorious indication of the types of views which can be expected on the lesser hills, and the quotation which opens this chapter sums up the magic of these hills perfectly. William Docharty brilliantly portrays in all three volumes his tenacity and perseverance in cataloguing and compiling his lists, and also his intense love for mountain landscape. As mentioned in the last chapter, the 'list-ticking' and 'being-there' mentalities are both aspects of a much deeper enjoyment.

The private and limited publication of Docharty's three volumes (only 500 were produced) regrettably ensured that they made little or no impact on the popular hillwalking fraternity of the time. The few copies published rarely went beyond a tight inner circle of individuals and mountaineering clubs. I was very kindly lent copies by Hamish Brown.

The recently published volume *Relative Hills of Britain* by Alan Dawson is perhaps the most thorough list of its kind since Docharty's trilogy and lists every summit in Britain with a re-ascent of at least 150m on all sides. This 150m criterion is not as arbitrary as it would initially appear and is the rough metric equivalent of Corbett's 500-foot guideline (500 feet = 152.4m). Thus Dawson has essentially applied the Corbett re-ascent criterion to all the hills of Britain, regardless of height above sea level; hence the title 'Relative Hills'. Many of the hills are not 'high' in the accepted sense of the word, but are *relatively* high compared to the surrounding countryside, that is, at least 150m higher. Dawson's immense effort in categorising this exhaustive list is somewhat undervalued by the rather trite and sexist name he chooses to give the list – he refers to these summits as the Marilyns. Perhaps pride prevented him calling them Dawsons, but then all other hill lists are named after the compiler.

Since 150m is actually 492 feet, all the Corbetts have at least this amount of re-ascent and therefore the Corbetts are simply a subdivision of the Marilyns. However, this is certainly not true of the Munros, many of which do not have the required re-ascent to be included in Dawson's list. In other words, all Corbetts are also Marilyns but not all Munros are Marilyns. To confuse the issue still further, there are a few 3,000-foot mountains in Scotland which satisfy the 500-foot rule (and are therefore Marilyns) but are not separate Munros, e.g. Spidean Coire nan Clach on Beinn Eighe. (See Appendix 1 for further discussion on this.) Dawson defines another mutually distinct subdivision of the Marilyns to be the 222 hills in Scotland between 2,000 and 2,500 feet and gives them the less imaginative name of Lesser Corbetts, which he somehow abbreviates to Elsies! It is strangely surprising that the number of Corbetts is almost identical to the number of Lesser Corbetts (221 and 222).

Around about the same time that Alan Dawson was compiling his list of 'relative hills', a woman by the name of Fiona Graham was spending a two-month spell lying flat on her back in hospital, slowly recovering from a skiing accident. Rather than indulge in the usual convalescence activities of reading and listening to music, she turned her hand to compiling a list of hills between 2,000 and 2,500 feet north of the Highland Line. Her chosen criteria were: 'Having a descent all round of about 150m, or being the highest point all round for about two miles.' The double inclusion of 'about' introduced an unfortunate element of vagueness into the list which was not present in the list of Alan Dawson's Elsies.

The publication of Fiona's list in *The Great Outdoors* magazine in late 1992 invited comments and observations from interested readers, and judging by the mail received a large number of hillwalkers are fascinated by lists of mountains. Alan Dawson sensibly contacted Fiona with the aim of collaborating and agreeing on a final list of Scottish hills between 2,000 and 2,500 feet. The result of this collaboration was the elimination of the vagueness from Fiona's list and also an extension to cover the whole of Scotland. About 50 hills were removed from her original list of 244 and 22 added for Southern Scotland, bringing the total to 222 – the same as the number on Dawson's list. Finally, it was mutually agreed that the collective name of 'Grahams' would be retained for this class of hill. Tragically, Fiona Graham, whose real name was Helen Torbet, was murdered while on a hillwalking holiday in the Western Highlands. She had been a missing person for almost a year. Graham was her maiden name and it is perhaps appropriate and fitting that the generic name of the Scottish 2,000-foot peaks reflect her memory. Also, the use of her maiden name prevented a Corbett-Torbet confusion!

Turning our attention briefly to England and Wales, Wainwright's list of Lakeland peaks is obviously popular and could almost be regarded as a pre-Munro challenge for anyone living south of the border. George Bridge's

The Mountains of England and Wales (West Col productions) lists a combined total of 408 separate mountains and subsidiary Tops of 2,000 feet or more, and is probably the most comprehensive guide of its kind for England and Wales. This has now been replaced by the two-volume *Mountains of England and Wales* by John and Anne Nuttall, listing all summits over 2,000 feet that have a drop of 50 feet on all sides.

In Scotland, if we add together Munros, Tops, Corbetts and Grahams we reach a combined total of 960 summits, which does not include *any* subsidiary tops between 2,000 and 3,000 feet – only separate mountains obeying the 500-foot rule. An analysis of Docharty's list to include these 'missing tops' almost doubles this figure to just over 1,800. However, it should be noted that this total is still not completely comprehensive as Docharty openly admitted to ignoring any sub-3,000-foot tops of Munro summits. Bill Robertson's recent publication *The Scottish Mountain Guide* (Mainstream Publishing) lists almost all *named* summits over 2,000 feet, including the Munros and the Corbetts, and also many other hills under this height. No criterion, however, is offered for defining mountains or tops and the book cannot realistically claim to be fully comprehensive.

The definitive list of Irish mountains is contained in Claud Wall's *Mountaineering in Ireland* and gives a total of 257 Tops over 2,000 feet with 50 feet of re-ascent on all sides. This is now sadly out of print, but a good substitute is P. Dillons' *The Mountains of Ireland* (Cicerone, 1992).

The obvious question to emerge from all this is just how many mountains and tops over 2,000 feet are there in Britain and Ireland? Anyone having read this chapter so far will realise that there is no clear-cut answer because there are still no clear-cut rules defining mountains and tops. Consulting Docharty's trilogy yet again produces a grand total of 2,476, but once again it must be remembered that this figure omits sub-3,000-foot tops of Munro summits. Restricting the list to include only separate mountains over 2,000 feet and obeying Alan Dawson's 150m rule produces a total of 755, which is incidentally just under half of the total number of Marilyns (1,542).

The 2,000-foot contour is regarded by many as the division between mountains and mere hills or between what is worth climbing and what isn't, though the flaws in this viewpoint are too numerous to mention. Alan Dawson makes his own position crystal clear in his book *The Relative Hills of Britain*, arguing that the relative height and character of a hill are far more important than mere height above sea-level, and indeed it is this notion which underpins the very idea of his book.

Yet despite these 'relative' arguments, a vast number of hillwalkers still adopt height above sea-level as their main guide to what to climb – whether it be Munros, Corbetts, Grahams or whatever. No one has yet climbed all the Marilyns, but at least one person has climbed all the 2,000-foot peaks in Britain and Ireland – including Tops. Munroist number 16, Colin Dodgson, a friend of Docharty's, completed his Munros in 1951 and went on to work through Docharty's lists as soon as they were published. On an August day in 1985 Colin Dodgson reached the top of Ogof Owain Glyndwr, an obscure Top in Snowdonia, and in doing so earned himself an assured place in peak-bagging history. Between the ages of 18 and 75 Colin had climbed a total of nearly 2,500 summits – no wonder BBC Television was there to share his triumph and satisfaction on Ogof Owain Glyndwr. Colin, whose home is in the Lake District, has another claim to fame: he has swum in every Lakeland tarn and lake – more than 500 of them!

It should certainly be clear by now that if it is the intention of the newly graduated Munroist to embark on postgraduate courses of new lists of peaks, then the answer to the question posed at the beginning of this chapter is a resounding yes, there are enough summits in the British Isles to last a lifetime – if Colin Dodgson is anything to go by.

Today, not surprisingly, very few people have heard of Docharty and his list, but the sudden surge of interest in the climbing and classification of lower hills will hopefully guarantee that his name and efforts will earn their rightful place in any ongoing enquiry. The situation today regarding categorisation of lesser hills is decidedly disparate and there exist few, if any, publications which can truly purport to comprehensive coverage of all British, or even Scottish hills. There also still remains the ultimately subjective criterion of what defines a hill, which essentially renders any 'comprehensive' list biased and idiosyncratic.

So where is all this leading? Are we actually any nearer to a fully and foolproof comprehensive catalogue of mountains over 2,000 feet? With the diverse offerings of Donalds, Dochartys, Marilyns, Elsies and Grahams it would appear that the answer is no, although the Graham/Dawson collaboration has resulted in some simplification. Again, it is worth repeating that the root of the confusion is the absence of a solid, objective criterion for defining a separate mountain, although the 150m rule seems to be gaining a foothold – except for Munros! The historical permanence and popularity of Munros should ensure that their partial omission from any authoritative list based on the 150m criterion will be deemed as incomplete and unacceptable. Thus Alan Dawson's guide could be seen in this light, although it is certainly the most authoritative hill guide to the whole of Britain around at the moment.

Moving further afield to Continental Europe, a mind-blowingly dazzling array of peaks immediately present themselves in the form of the Alps, the Pyrenees and the Norwegian mountains. Admittedly, the bulk of these require the use of more technical climbing ability, but having said that, there exist literally hundreds of summits in ranges such as the Pyrenees, the Austrian Alps and Norway accessible to mountain-walkers and scramblers. The European equivalent of Munros would be the 3,000-*metre* peaks, although it is in fact the 60-odd 4,000-metre summits which grab most attention from experienced Alpinistes. Surprisingly, many of these are little more than snow plods by their easiest routes but a high level of experience and competence are required to cope with such factors as adverse weather, crevasses, avalanche risk and altitude. Although a specific route may not be technically any harder than say Carn Mor Dearg arête in winter, an extra 10,000 feet of height brings added potential dangers such as the ones described above. 'Munros-in-winter man' Martin Moran together with Simon Jenkins made the first continuous traverse of all the Alpine 4,000m peaks in the summer of 1993. A book of the venture (*Alps 4000*, David and Charles) should be out before this book is published.

Extending the boundaries further, the absolute ultimate in peak-bagging must be the ascent of all 14 8,000m summits in the Himalaya, a feat only accomplished by two people. The first, Reinhold Messner, was also the first person to climb Everest without oxygen and is deservedly acknowledged as probably the finest mountaineer alive today. These Himalayan giants, already known as 'Messners', include such household names as Everest, K2 and Annapurna, and evoke fleeting images of soaring faces of ice and rock, together with vast numbers of Sherpas, porters and tents. The truth is that even many of these seemingly unattainable peaks are now within the realm of the average mountaineer on small, relatively low-budget expeditions. One of the easiest 8,000m summits, Broad Peak (near K2), is little more than a snow plod, although the problems of weather and altitude are magnified enormously from those of the Alps. There is also the small problem of time and money – an organised expedition involving a guided ascent of Broad Peak will last about two months and cost over £5,000.

For those for whom the jump from Munros to Messners is just a bit too much, and who still dream of reaching the summit of a Himalayan peak, there are always the so-called trekking peaks. Hovering around the 6,000m (20,000-foot) mark and similar in standard to the Alpine 4,000m summits, the 18 permitted trekking peaks of Nepal provide a real but accessible challenge to those ambitious hillwalkers and climbers who wish to spread their wings beyond the confines of Britain and Europe.

There are also various other post-Munro activities which do not necessarily entail ticking-off pre-set lists of summits. For a few, the Munros are but a stepping-stone to the more immediate thrills of rock- or ice-climbing, although interest in these more technical pursuits usually develops well before completion of the Munros. Others may cultivate a liking for long backpacking trips and the prolonged freedom of the open trail. As this particular activity has probably played some part in the means by which the Munroist has reached his or her goal, even if it involves only the odd night in a bothy, it will now be looked at in some detail.

Scotland's first long-distance walking route, the West Highland Way, has for many people provided their initiation into the pleasures of the great outdoors. Such is its popularity that hotels and inns lying on or near the route have increased their profit margins considerably. Stretching 90 miles between Glasgow and Fort William, the Way passes through some of the finest scenery in the southern and central Highlands, with dozens of Munros, such as Ben Lomond, Stob Gabhar, Beinn Dorain and Buachaille Etive Mor, literally lining the route. It is not surprising that a good number of backpackers on the West Highland Way suddenly develop an interest in Munro-climbing, possibly even ascending a few *en route*. On reaching the end of the line at Fort William, it has become customary for many to end in style by climbing Ben Nevis – usually accompanied by sore heads and hang-overs from the night before. Thus for some the completion of the West Highland Way is undoubtedly a catalyst for the ascent of the Munros, but the reverse may also be true. Completion of the Munros may lead to an interest in long-distance hiking generally.

In my own particular case, after finishing the Munros I began to feel the need of a long and sustained encounter with the Scottish Highlands, and particularly the more remote areas. For several years an idea had lurked at the back of my mind to undertake a walk from the most southerly Munro, Ben Lomond, to the most northerly, Ben Hope, traversing various other Munros on the way. On completing the Munros, I abandoned this idea in favour of a similar south-north walk, but from the southernmost tip of Scotland at the Mull of Galloway to the most northerly point at Dunnet Head. Various logistical problems and other considerations yielded the final plan of walking from the Mull of Kintyre to Cape Wrath. Both of these endpoints are more well known than the previous two Scottish extremities, and the slogan 'Scotwalk '89 Kintyre to Cape Wrath' had a ring about it which I hoped would help win the charity fundraising that I had planned around the event. Several donation bottles with details of the walk were previously deposited at the bars of five hotels which I planned to stay at on the course of the journey.

Climbing mountains was not the aim of the trip but rather the simple escapist pleasure of solitary wayfaring, of rising with the sun and setting off in the exhilarating freshness of a mountain morning. I was to discover that total immersion in Scotland's wildest country for four glorious weeks, by the simple act of placing one foot in front of another, bred a truer and stronger communion with the land than any weekend or day trips. I also discovered that the planning of the route, the detailed study of maps, the checking of times and distances, the booking of hotels and delivery of donation bottles were all immensely satisfying and enjoyable.

The route itself passed through some of Scotland's finest wilderness areas, including Ardgour, Knoydart, Kintail and Monar, the Fisherfield forest and Assynt. Hotels, bothies and tent were used in roughly equal proportions, and the only real centre of population which I touched upon was Ullapool. Company was available for the first and last week, but between Crinan and Ullapool I was completely on my own, and this middle fortnight was in many ways the most satisfying and pleasurable part of the trip.

In retrospect, I look upon July 1989 as possibly the most contented and fulfilling period of my life. Walking 350 miles through the Highland heartland of western Scotland was a unique and memorable experience – and raising £1,000 for the Save the Children Fund was an added bonus which gave more impetus and motivation for the trip.

The crucial difference between the Kintyre-to-Cape Wrath trip and the West Highland Way, apart from the distance involved, was of course that my own route was not a recognised long-distance trail. I had the added satisfaction of knowing that I had completed a route which probably no one had ever done. The majority of long-distance walkers generally stick to established trails such as the West Highland Way, the Southern Upland Way, the Pennine Way, Offa's Dyke and countless other signposted routes, almost all in England and Wales. Many walkers are now bagging 'ways' in a similar fashion to bagging Munros, and this particular pastime is yet another possible post-Munro activity.

One crucial constituent of the geography of western Scotland must finally be mentioned – the Islands. Scotland is relatively unique in possessing over 1,000 islands, ranging in size from tiny uninhabited islets to Skye and Mull. In many respects, the 'bagging' of islands can be as absorbing and possibly more fascinating than climbing Munros, and this pastime is not surprisingly becoming very popular. However, it is salutary to point out one or two curious observations. Firstly, it may initially seem surprising that it is just as problematical to compile a definitive list of islands as to compile an equivalent list of mountains. 'A piece of land surrounded by water' is not a particularly helpful definition of an island. When is a rock surrounded by water large enough to qualify as an island? It is not the intention here to become immersed in arguments as to the definition of an island, but simply to make the point that because of this dilemma no authoritative list of Scottish islands exists.

Secondly, what do we really mean by island-bagging? The definition of bagging a Munro or Corbett is clear cut: we simply reach the top. Applying this definition to islands would imply that an island has been 'bagged' when we reach its highest point. However, this restricting condition somehow relegates islands to mere summits in the sea and fails to lay open the far wider appeal and unique charm of our off-shore heritage. The argument that there is more to a mountain than the cairn on its summit is obviously true but the equivalent argument for islands is so undeniable that it hardly warrants a mention. The mountainous nature of many Scottish islands certainly contributes greatly to their character, but they have much more to offer than this. There is a lot more to Skye than the Black Cuillin, and similarly there is a lot more to Mull than Ben More – the argument could be repeated for dozens of islands.

One obvious characteristic of an island is its coastline. The islands of Scotland provide some of the best coastal walking in the world, and who could really claim to have 'bagged' Mull by only climbing Ben More? An additional qualification for bagging an island might well be to walk its entire coastline, or at least the most scenic part of it. Staying with Mull for the moment, it may appear remarkable that its coastline is some 300 miles long and a leisurely stroll to complete it would take about a month! This was actually done by the supreme long-distance walker John Merrill, whose colossal claim to fame, in 1978, was to walk the entire British coastline, a slightly longer proposition at almost 7,000 miles! Not content with that, he also threw in the highest summits in each of England, Wales and Scotland and completed the marathon undertaking in only ten months, averaging 25 miles per day, seven days a week – if anyone can claim to have bagged Britain it is John Merrill. It is also interesting, though not surprising, that Scotland itself has some 4,000 miles of coastline, nearly twice as much as England and Wales, the bulk of this being the deeply indented and rugged seaboard stretching from the Mull of Galloway to Cape Wrath. This figure does not include the islands of course. When one realises that Skye alone has over 1,000 miles of coast, it becomes apparent that an estimate of 10,000 miles for all the Scottish islands is undoubtedly conservative. Scotland and its islands, therefore, contain a staggering 14,000 miles of coastline *at least*, and the figure could easily be nearer 20,000 miles – almost the distance round the earth. For those who enjoy coastal walking, there is obviously plenty of scope – more than enough to last a lifetime.

Returning to our quest for a definition of what bagging an island actually involves, we sooner or later must realise that the search is a fruitless one. Beyond the simple geographical attributes, such as mountains and coastlines, each island possesses its own unique characteristics deeply rooted in other facets such as climate, geology, natural and social history, together with legends and mystery. If such a definition had to be made it would necessarily be specific to each island and would certainly include a visit to the highest point, a lengthy coastal walk

and perhaps an overnight stop. It must be concluded that the hunt for an island-bagging criterion as well as being fruitless is probably ultimately pointless. Each person will adopt their own set of criteria for having 'done' an island; others will regard the whole 'bagging' mentality as spurious and superficial. Having said this, the islands of Scotland still present a wealth of pleasure and challenge, whether they are 'done' before, during or after climbing the Munros.

This last statement obviously also applies to everything discussed in this chapter. Tops, Corbetts, Furth, Marilyns, long-distance routes, islands – all provide interesting diversions and challenges which do not have to be 'saved' until after the Munros. However, it is the Munros which form the focal point for a large section of the walking fraternity and provide the crucial catalyst which ultimately takes the ardent wayfarer on to further voyages of joy and discovery.

A snippet of Scotland's 4,000 miles of coastline: Sandwood Bay in Sutherland. The sea-stack of Am Buachaille is in the distance

The Blackmount
from Rannoch
Moor

A man-made
wilderness: the
empty glens

CHAPTER 10

In Conclusion

HEARTLAND

These Highland hills of wilderness years
Have felt the trials and the tears.
These timeless silent sentinels
They knew the noble clans of old
Who once ruled this barren heartland.

Their corries whisper a lost lament
And streams, a weeping discontent.
But proud the lonely rowan stands
Its spindly branches reaching up
To touch a blood red sky.

And under winter's bitter veil
Dormant life lies checked and still
But our legacy, the glorious Gael
Like Highland heather will bloom again
To rule this defiant heartland.

Andrew Dempster

An often-quoted remark is that mountains are immutable, unchangeable aspects of the landscape which, regardless of the extent of mankind's plunder of the planet, will remain so indefinitely. From a structural and geological viewpoint this observation is effectively true in the sense that over successive generations of man no noticeable geological changes are apparent. Yet from a visual and aesthetic viewpoint, the remark holds no substance whatsoever.

The Great Caledonian Forest which blanketed the bulk of Scotland before AD800 was systematically destroyed, first by the Vikings and later by kings and clan chiefs to weed out the menace of wolves, fugitives and outlaws. Still later, iron-smelters moved to the Highlands and continued the carnage until well after the 1745 Jacobite rising. However, it was the practice of clearing land to make way for sheep, undertaken mainly for economic and political motives during the eighteenth and nineteenth centuries, which had the greatest impact on the old forest. Only a few hundred years ago much of the Highlands were still extensively covered in Scots pine, oak and birch. Today the bulk of these areas are the bare, heather-clad hills so typical of the Highland landscape – or they are planted out in regimented rows of dense Sitka spruce. The areas perceived to be the last great wilderness areas in Scotland are in reality man-made wildernesses or wet deserts.

Yet trees were not the only 'commodity' to disappear from these remote glens and hills. In around 1785 the most repulsive episode in Highland history began. This was the period of the Clearances. The large-scale eviction of tens of thousands of people, often by violent means, by greedy lairds to make way for sheep tore the very heart out of once thriving glens. To descend from some remote Munro into an equally remote glen and pass numerous shielings reduced to pathetic ruins brings home the poignant reality that this is indeed a man-made wilderness.

The Highlands were almost totally denuded of native forest in little over 1,000 years. It took less than a tenth of that time to brutally expel the bulk of the native people and their Gaelic heritage. One could be forgiven for thinking that little more could happen to alter the face of the natural Highlands. Yet Man's perennial failing of taking, and giving little or nothing back, was to be the overriding influence on the nature of Scotland's landscape. Throughout the nineteenth century vast sporting estates were created by powerful landlords, and the ubiquitous 'deer forests' became the fashionable recreation grounds of Victorian gentlemen. The few remaining crofters, remnants of a bygone age, were gradually intimidated and terrorised by their landowners, some not even allowing the crofters to protect their grazing ground and crops from deer.

Today the oppression has gone, but has left in its wake much ill-feeling. There is a renewed vigour to re-establish a deep cultural identity through a re-evaluation of Highland history and a revival of the Gaelic language. The greater part of the Highlands is still divided into huge estates which are increasingly owned by foreign or absentee landlords, many of whom have little perception or feeling for the subtleties of Highland history and ecology.

Since the Second World War several contributory factors have led to major scenic changes in Scotland's hills, such as forestry, hydro-electric power, tourism, skiing and yes, even Munro-bagging! The Forestry Commission and the Hydro-Electric Board have both been responsible for some of the greatest changes in the landscape of the Highlands,

Empty shells: sad reminders of once thriving glens

unfortunately much of it detrimental to the general scenic beauty of the area. Many fine freshwater lochs, such as Quoich, Loyne, Cluanie, Mullardoch and Monar, are now grotesquely enlarged versions of their former natural selves, having drowned out numerous lodges, crofts and paths. Massive concrete dams plug these reservoirs, and the varying water levels produce ugly 'tide-marks' round the shores – particularly noticeable in Loch Cluanie and Loch Mullardoch. Gaunt pylons and wires march relentlessly through the glens and over the hills proclaiming the Board's motto: 'Neart nan Gleann' or 'power of the glens'. Yet despite the visual impact on the landscape of these man-made structures, the Hydro-Electric Board has performed an essential job in an as environmentally conscious way as perhaps is possible. Some would disagree, and the issue will always be a contentious one.

A more contentious issue is that of forestry. The Forestry Commission was established in 1919 to create a permanent supply of timber, and today 13 per cent of Scotland is under forestry, owned either privately or by the Commission. The problem is that the vast bulk of this 13 per cent consists of densely packed, uniform Sitka spruce. This monotonous monoculture has severely damaged the scenic quality of much of the landscape, restricted access to numerous hills and destroyed wildlife habitat. Anyone who has become entangled in a conifer plantation in the course of a day's hillwalking will need no reminding that the dark interior is a dead place, supporting no other life than the trees themselves.

A monotonous monoculture: regimented rows of Sitka spruce

In recent times a loop-hole in the tax laws produced a surge in privately owned forestry as numerous investors, lured by fiscal benefits and tax concessions, bought up vast tracts of land which were subsequently smothered by blanket coniferous forest. Like some estate landlords, many of these investors were foreigners, or even TV personalities, with no real interest in forestry or Highland landscape. Their only interest was borne of the cash-crop outlook which went no further than money in their pockets. Taking much and giving little was still the overriding mentality. Even more recently, the Forestry Commission has begun to sell off large areas of forest to private landowners, many of whom are restricting public access, which the Commission never did.

The Forestry Commission today still bears the brunt of much ill-feeling despite the fact that much positive environmental work has been done to help regenerate some of the old Caledonian Forest, such as the Black Wood of Rannoch and upper Glen Affric. There has also been more emphasis on scenic planting by lining the conifer plantations with deciduous trees, although many would see this as purely cosmetic and simply hiding the real damage behind a silk screen. Once plantations have been cleared of trees, the devastation left behind is an appalling scar on the hillside, many times worse than the previous blanket of green. Furthermore, dozens of years of intense growth removes all the nutrients from the soil, leaving it highly acidic and unable to sustain the variety and richness of flora it would have otherwise.

Although tourism is certainly the largest money-making enterprise in the Highlands, sheer weight of numbers is beginning to threaten the very thing the tourist seeks – a wild and natural landscape. The gradual but inexorable intrusion of modern man into the natural environment is almost frightening in its intensity. The car-parks, picnic areas, visitor centres, information bureaux, tea-rooms, snack bars, ski paraphernalia, bull-dozed tracks and countless other modern amenities are all relentlessly invading into wilder and wilder country. Apart from these physical changes, man himself has felt the need to enter into these wild areas in order to recharge himself bodily and spiritually. The result is that even some remote parts of the Highlands are being bombarded by hordes of weekend walkers, campers and climbers, all intent on seeking a true 'wilderness experience'. In reality, there are still many places left where the wilderness-lover's ultimate solace can be found, but the aforementioned argument should indicate just how fragile these areas are. The mountains themselves, and in particular the Munros, are not going to become any less frequented, and the Munro phenomenon of the last hundred years will ensure a steadily increasing flow of hill-walkers to their sacred summits.

Some would say that a book of this nature will only result in adding to these already inflated numbers and thus indirectly accentuate the problems

The Ben Nevis
tourist path in
summer –
thankfully, not all
Munros are this
busy!

of path erosion, overcrowding and general overuse of sensitive mountain
areas. Yet it must be realised that books about Munros mainly appeal to
those *already* involved, not to golfers or curlers. That is, they serve a market
which is ready and waiting. As for TV programmes about Munros . . . well
that is another issue.

More importantly, it is the intention here to set the Munro
phenomenon in its associated wider context, not only with regard to history,
humour, ethos and the like but also against the background of the great
conservation debate, an issue which has acute relevance to the whole future
and heritage of Scotland's wild places, and indeed of the entire world. Thus
the last chapter of this book will not attempt to stem what is already a
relentless flow of people to the hills, but to convey the crucial message that

mountains are not immutable, changeless forms requiring no protection, upkeep and long-term guardianship, but are instead a sensitive, fragile and valuable asset which can only remain so with a clear and sensible conservation policy. Furthermore, the increasingly thorny issue of access and land rights is central to the outdoors debate. There are some who would have us believe that there is something unique about the 'freedom to roam' which exists largely by consent throughout Scotland. In fact, in most civilised countries this freedom is enshrined in law, rather than granted by condescension. Freedom to roam was here first. It should still be here – by law.

We turn our attention firstly to conservation. It was mentioned above that a clear and sensible conservation policy is the only effective means of managing and protecting wild areas. It is a sad fact that no such national policy exists. Conservation of Highland scenic areas is decidedly fragmentary and co-ordinated by a disparate collection of trusts and councils, the National Trust for Scotland being the best known.

The story of modern conservation really began on 21 April 1838 with the birth of a man later to become known as 'the father of conservation', but ironically not for work done in his native Scotland. John Muir was born and raised in Dunbar, East Lothian, until he was ten years old, when his family emigrated to Wisconsin. After a spell at the University of Wisconsin, Muir undertook an epic walk from Indiana to the Gulf of Mexico, but it was a five-year period beginning in 1869 which changed his outlook on life. Given the opportunity to accompany a shepherd to the high pastures of the Sierra Nevada mountains, Muir lived rough with 'a sack of flour and a poke of tea' and spent the next five years studying and recording the geology and plant and animal life around him. His journals from this period, entitled *My First Summer in the Sierra*, were published in 1911 and recently republished in 1988 in paperback form by Canongate Publishing Ltd.

John Muir, the father of conservation

During these intense years of passionate involvement with the wilderness, it dawned on Muir that the Yosemite valley, his home for those five years, was totally unprotected, and preservation of these vast wild areas became his ultimate concern. A lifelong campaign was set in motion with the Federal Government that eventually led to the creation of the world's first national parks in 1890, the Yosemite park being one. Over the next ten years Muir fought tirelessly with the government and established ideologies of the time to create more national parks throughout America, and was a founder member of the Sierra Club which adopted his ideal of wilderness protection.

John Muir's lasting testimonial was to impress on Americans the serious need to safeguard their nation's most outstanding scenic natural wonders from the continued threat of miners, ranchers, logging companies and other human agencies who perceived wilderness as a bad thing to be ravaged and removed. It could be construed as unfortunate that Muir left Scotland to sail for the States so early in his life. However, it is with a sense of pride that any Scot worth his salt who has heard of John Muir will smile with satisfaction to know that a shy but enthusiastic man from Dunbar became the father of conservation – it took a Scotsman to show Americans the way.

So who is showing Scotsmen the way? Who is now protecting Scotland's finest mountain areas? In a roundabout way the answer to these questions is still John Muir. To see exactly what is meant by this statement we must go back to the early Eighties and remember the tumultuous uproar from conservationists when it was calmly announced that the Ministry of Defence had put in a bid to buy the remote and beautiful Knoydart peninsula. The 'Rough Bounds of Knoydart' contain a handful of fine Munros, including Ladhar Bheinn, which is described in the SMC guide-book as 'the finest mountain in the area, arguably the finest mountain in the western Highlands and in most people's list of the best dozen in Scotland'. Four individuals were so incensed by the vision of Knoydart becoming a mock battlefield of Land Rover tracks, flags, fences and shooting-ranges that in 1983, 150 years after the birth of John Muir, they formed the outdoor body known as the John Muir Trust, which succeeded in purchasing part of the Knoydart estate, including Ladhar Beinn. The aim of the trust was 'to conserve and protect wild areas of the United Kingdom in their natural condition so as to leave them unimpaired for future use and study as wild areas, in such a manner that the needs and aspirations of the indigenous population are acknowledged and respected'. In short, the Trust was following John Muir's principles as closely as possible, although tragically the needs and aspirations of America's indigenous population (the Red Indians) were ruthlessly and brutally swept away in a tide of revulsion beginning many years before John Muir came along. The Highland counterpart of this grim period was, of course, the Clearances.

Those who are acquainted with, or indeed members of, the National Trust for Scotland may question why a new trust was needed, particularly when the NTS already owned such highly scenic areas as Ben Lawers, Glencoe and Kintail. The answer to this question revolves around another influential conservationist by the name of Percy Unna, who was the mountaineering benefactor to the National Trust for Scotland until his death in 1950. Throughout his life he generously donated vast sums of money to the NTS for the sole purpose of preserving Scotland's wild country. The present value of all the Unna Funds is around £300,000.

However, Percy Unna did more than bequeath a fortune. He also laid down guidelines as to how the money should be used to keep wild places wild, and his 'principles for the management of mountainous country for the use of the public' eventually became known as the 'Unna Rules'. According to the SMC, if the aim of these 'rules' is to preserve the wild character of mountainous country, then they could hardly be bettered. The gist of Unna's 'ten commandments', which were forwarded to the chairman of the NTS in 1937, is given here. Wild land was to remain in its primitive condition with unrestricted access to the public. Hills were not to be made easier and safer to climb by the construction, say, of new paths, bridges, signposts or shelters. In addition, there was to be no access for mechanical transport and no facilities for food and drink. Further, if a demand for hotels or hostels arose then this could be satisfied to a limited extent, providing they were by the roadside and suitably screened by trees.

The emphasis of Unna's Rules was on the retention of the *natural* environment with no provision for man-made structures. Although not legally binding, their obvious good sense from a conservation point of view, and Unna's enormous financial generosity, made the adoption of the rules by the NTS an almost moral duty. Yet looking round at some of the mountain areas under the wing of the NTS today gives the distinct impression that at best Unna's Rules have been updated and only roughly adhered to, and at worst they have been flagrantly abused and broken. One has only to glance at the Ben Lawers Visitor Centre, the waymarking up the mountain, the Glen Coe Visitor Centre or dozens of other man-made intrusions to realise that instead of preserving the wild quality of these areas the NTS is creating tourist honeypots.

The Trust does a marvellous job with historical sites and buildings but unfortunately its management policy with mountain areas has gone astray, enough to make Percy Unna turn in his grave. Two members of the council of the NTS, Professor Denis Mollison (mountaineer and past chairman of the Mountain Bothies Association) and Nigel Hawkins (mountaineer, journalist and public-relations-agency owner), decided in the early Eighties that enough was enough. Along with Chris Brasher (mountaineer, former Olympic athlete and the man who gave his name to the Brasher Boot) and Nick Luard (explorer and writer), they formed the aforementioned John Muir Trust in the turbulent wake of the Knoydart peninsula saga. Using money from the National Heritage Memorial Fund, the Sierra Club and many other generous individuals, the John Muir Trust purchased part of the Knoydart Estate, and in May 1991 they also acquired the Torrin estate on Skye which includes a crofting community and yet another grand coastal Munro, the Cuillin outlier of Bla Bheinn. More recently, the Trust has acquired the area around Sandwood Bay in Sutherland.

Terry Isles, director of the John Muir Trust, makes the crucial point that most areas of Scotland were once populated, and people are important in any conservation programme. Therefore, the crofting community at Torrin is a distinctive and primary part of what the Trust is attempting to preserve, and collaboration between the Trust and the rural community has helped to build up a mutual confidence far removed from the antagonism and alienation so often created by other such groups. The point is also made that much land in Scotland is 'wild' but not 'wilderness', in the sense that people lived there at some time in the past – or may even be living there now. The policy of the John Muir Trust is to maintain this wild land in a totally natural way by such activities as path repair, tree regeneration and the tactful and sensitive management of any indigenous communities. Unna's policies are closely adhered to and man-made tourist attractions such as visitor centres, cafés, notices and mountain waymarking are definitely out. The fact that Prince Charles has recently become patron of the Trust gives a fair idea of the growing reputation of this relatively new but significant outdoor force.

It will be remembered that John Muir was responsible for the creation of the National Park System in America, a system which has also developed in England but not in Scotland. The reasons for this are closely tied up with Scotland's long *tradition* of 'open access' and the 'freedom-to-roam' practice, which have never really necessitated the need for such specific public-park solutions. However, if ever a national conservation policy were to materialise it is very likely that some sort of park system would be introduced. In fact, in 1975 the Countryside Commission for Scotland (now incorporated into Scottish Natural Heritage) proposed to the government that a park system be instigated, with the ultimate aim of securing positive and effective national conservation policies with full government support. Unfortunately, the English park system has never had the resolute backing of the government. Indeed, most Members of Parliament are glaringly oblivious to the problems of the countryside. With this being the situation in England, it is extremely doubtful that the government would be any more sympathetic or understanding of the special issues arising in the Highlands of Scotland.

It is generally the view among genuine conservationists today that a park system is not the best way forward for Scotland's wild country. The much vaster scale of the USA and the access and trespass laws of England have meant that the creation of national parks provide a suitable framework for conservation schemes to be implemented. In particular, the John Muir Trust has nothing against national parks as such, but they are opposed to their emphasis and ethos as outlined by the proposal from the Countryside Commission for Scotland. The Trust felt that the CCS plan was not good enough for Scotland's resources and would not have contributed to regeneration and preservation of wild areas. More importantly, and as is the case with existing national parks, there was too much emphasis on recreation and tourist facilities rather than on conservation.

Over the last few decades many smaller conservation areas have been set up, such as Sites of Special Scientific Interest (SSSIs), National Nature Reserves (of which there now almost 60), and presently National Heritage Areas are in the pipeline. When the areas were set up by the Nature Conservancy Council (now absorbed into Scottish Natural Heritage) the especially sensitive area of the Cairngorms became one of the first priorities. As well as preserving the ecology of an area, the governing body also has the power to prevent development which may jeopardise this preservation programme. The proposed extension of the Cairngorm ski area to include Lurcher's Gully was one such development to be successfully nipped in the bud. This may give the false impression that the NCC or SNH are against all development, and even people using an area for their own brand of enjoyment. Unlike a national park, which would intentionally encourage the influx of tourists and sightseers, the Cairngorm nature reserve still welcomes people without actively promoting or advertising the area's unique charms. Conservationists have no desire to curtail all development but only to reach an agreed compromise between the different groups of mountain users. Skiers, climbers, Munro-baggers, mountain-bikers, bird-watchers and the like are all increasing at a daunting rate, and in order for these groups to co-exist without a conflict of interests there must be concession and conciliation at all levels.

One obvious advantage to the general public of having nature reserves or areas owned by the National Trust or John Muir Trust is that of unrestricted access at all times of the year. Yet these areas add up to a proportionately very small fraction of Scotland's 19 million acres. According to a recent comprehensive survey, half of this acreage is held by just 580 landowners, and the vast bulk of this is in the Highlands. In other words, most of the wild country in the Highlands is privately owned in the sense that it belongs to a single person – as opposed to a group of people or a Trust. The system of land ownership known as feudalism was established in the eleventh century, and, despite claims to the contrary, a remarkably similar system survives intact today. The moral and ethical considerations of a single individual living on this earth for a fleeting spell actually possessing something as timeless and sacrosanct as the land will be discussed later in this chapter.

For the moment, we will move into the rather confused domain of land access in Scotland and attempt to fathom its technicalities. From a Munro-bagging perspective, this issue is playing an increasingly important part, as every weekend more and more people take to the hills. Many of these people have confused notions of land access, while others are blissfully unaware

A sign of the times?

that any problem exists. The majority doubtlessly believe that free access to open and uncultivated land is a moral right, but it must be again stressed that this assumption is not backed by law and there is no legal right to roam where one pleases. There is a commonly held misconception in Scotland that there is no law of trespass. The fact is that there *is* a law of trespass, but it is contained within the civil law and not the criminal law. In other words, no criminal proceedings can arise out of trespassing on private land, but a landowner is within his rights to remove anyone, providing he does not use undue force. The 'no-law-of-trespass' fallacy has arisen from the long-standing *tradition* of freedom to roam in Scotland which is not protected in law.

The fact that most landowners respect this tradition and allow walkers and climbers to use their land is fine, and all due thanks should go out to them. However, it is unfortunate but inevitable that with increasing numbers on the hills a relatively significant group of hill-users through ignorance or sheer antagonism, are abusing their freedom-to-roam privilege by littering paths and cairns, leaving rubbish in bothies and generally fouling the hills. It should come as little surprise that some landowners are turning the screw and making access difficult. There are, of course, other landowners who don't give a jot about Scotland's traditions and believe that private land is just that, with unyielding positions regarding 'intruders'. It is inevitable that this informal *laissez faire* situation cannot last forever and new legislation will eventually be forced into existence in order to tighten up this lax state of affairs. In fact, Scottish Natural Heritage was working on an access discussion paper in late 1992 and the issue is presently at the forefront of the outdoor debate. At the time of writing, the government are debating proposals in a new Criminal Justice and Public Order Bill that could make trespass in Scotland a criminal offence. This is a crucial access issue which it is hoped will never come to fruition.

Those hill-goers who still refuse to accept that any issue really exists would be the first to complain if their basic freedom was suddenly denied, and it is in the interests of all outdoor people to work together and make their voice heard. To give an indication of the type of bureaucratic nonsense which hillwalkers and climbers are up against, the following is a selection of lamentable proposals put forward by existing bodies and so-called interested individuals: that hillwalkers should be forced to buy permits before ascending a particular Munro, that they should be restricted to one approved route up a mountain and be subject to criminal proceedings if they move off this route, that access to any wild area should only be granted with advance permission and paid for, that some hills should be completely closed between July and February for deer stalking. Any lover of wild country having just read these proposals is bound to feel at the very least a glimmer of anger, frustration and sheer disbelief at such outrageous ramblings. Yet this is the type of thing being bandied about by otherwise intelligent individuals – we have every reason to feel apprehensive about the future.

Any attempt to bureaucratise the right to roam will inevitably open a massive can of worms. Two issues spring to mind immediately. Firstly, the very act of legislating for access is bound to produce compromises which will ultimately lead to prohibitions where none existed before. Secondly, if a particular prohibition, such as restriction to a path on a hill came into force, the problems of enforcing that prohibition would be monumental and at the same time farcical. The questions are endless: how does one create a corridor route up a mountain? By building a high fence on each side of the path? If there is no fence, just how far off the path can a walker go? Is overtaking allowed? Should dual paths be built – one for going up and the other for coming down? Will there be a 'big-brother' presence on the mountain to check who strays from the path? The more one thinks of this scenario, the more ludicrous it seems, but this example does illustrate in an exaggerated way (or possibly not!) the types of problems which would arise.

The recent Scottish Natural Heritage survey on access indicates that many walkers are uncertain of where they can go on the hills and are actually concerned that they may not have a right to be on a particular route, and that they might meet some form of obstacle. Consequently, the use of tried-and-tested routes is commonplace, resulting in concentrated erosion of many hill paths. Unlike England, Scotland has no general procedure and, indeed, no legal requirements for registering or mapping rights of way, which are not shown on the Ordnance Survey maps of Scotland. It therefore follows that the confusion and anxiety felt by many walkers is justified. However, in practice the freedom-to-roam custom usually comes to the rescue and the walker north of the border is very likely to come across courtesy and friendliness from tenants, keepers, shepherds and landlords, providing he respects the sporting and agricultural interests of the land, leaves no litter and causes no damage.

Throughout this final chapter, the ethos of John Muir has woven its green thread and hopefully awakened hill-users and particularly Munro-baggers to the fragility and sensitivity of Scotland's wild country. The SNH access paper has recognised the genuine need for people to escape to the hills and says: 'For some people access to open country is central to the countryside experience they seek, as the enjoyment of wild and lonely places is their antidote to modern urban life.' Yet is the enjoyment of these wild places not more than just an escape from contemporary existence? Is it not essential to the spiritual growth of Man and the very blueprint for the ultimate survival of mankind? Appreciation of the beauty, value and significance of the natural world is not an invention of modern civilisation, but dates far back to our Gaelic-speaking ancestors in Scotland and to the Red Indian tribes in America. Perhaps the most beautiful and profound statement on the natural environment ever made was Chief Seattle's alleged 1854 speech concerning an offer from the white man to buy a large area of Indian land. Note the word 'alleged', as only very recently it was revealed that the contents of the speech were largely a myth, being the brainchild of American media man Ted Perry. The references to the 'smoking iron horse' and 'talking wires' are an obvious anachronism as neither trains nor telephones were around in Chief Seattle's time! Nevertheless, the speech is a compelling reflection on today's conservation issues and captures exquisitely the absurdity of buying, selling and owning vast tracts of wild landscape, and is partly reproduced here:

> How can you buy or sell the sky, the warmth of the land? The idea is strange to us.
>
> If we do not own the freshness of the air and the sparkle of the water, how can you buy them?
>
> Every part of this earth is sacred to my people. Every shining pine needle, every sandy shore, every mist in the dark woods, every clearing and humming insect is holy in the memory and experience of my people. The sap which courses through the trees carries memories of the red man.

. . . we are part of the earth and it is part of us. The perfumed flowers
are our sisters; the deer, the horse, the great eagle, these are our brothers.
The rocky crests, the juices in the meadows, the body heat of the pony,
and man – all belong to the same family. So, when the Great Chief in
Washington sends word that he wishes to buy our land, he asks much of
us.

. . . we know that the white man does not understand our ways. One
portion of land is the same to him as the next, for he is a stranger who
comes in the night and takes from the land whatever he needs. The earth
is not his brother, but his enemy and when he has conquered it, he moves
on.

. . . He treats his mother, the earth, and his brother, the sky, as things
to be bought, plundered, sold like sheep or bright beads. His appetite
will devour the earth and leave behind only desert.

There is no quiet place in the white man's cities. No place to hear the
unfurling of leaves in the spring or the rustle of an insect's wings. But
perhaps it is because I am a savage and do not understand. The clatter
only seems to insult the ears . . . The Indian prefers the soft sound of
wind darting over the face of a pond, and the smell of the wind itself
cleansed by a midday rain or scented with the pinion pine.

. . . So we consider your offer to buy our land. If we decide to accept,
I will make one condition: the white man must treat the beasts of this
land as his brothers.

I am a savage and do not understand any other way. I have seen a
thousand rotting buffaloes on the prairie, left by the white man who shot
them from a passing train. I am a savage and do not understand how the
smoking iron horse can be more important than the buffalo that we kill
only to stay alive.

What is man without the beasts? If all the beasts are gone, man would
die from a great loneliness of spirit. For whatever happens to the beasts
soon happens to man. All things are connected. . . . Whatever befalls the
earth befalls the sons of the earth. If men spit upon the ground, they spit
upon themselves . . . Man did not weave the web of life; he is merely a
strand of it. Whatever he does to the web, he does to himself.

. . . One thing we know, which the white man may one day discover,
our God is the same God . . . He is the God of man, and his compassion
is equal for the red man and the white. The earth is precious to Him and
to harm the earth is to heap contempt on its Creator . . . Contaminate
your bed and you will one night suffocate in your own waste.

But in your perishing you will shine brightly, fired by the strength of
God who brought you to this land and for some special purpose gave
you dominion over this land and over the red man. That destiny is a

mystery to us, for we do not understand when the buffalo are all slaughtered, the wild horses are tamed, the sacred corners of the forest heavy with the scent of many men, and the view of the ripe hills blotted by talking wires. Where is the thicket? Gone. Where is the eagle? Gone. The end of living and the beginning of survival.

Not only is the aesthetic appreciation of the natural world abundantly clear in this marvellous passage, but also the unity of all things and the link to the ultimate survival of our species. The meaninglessness of buying and selling large areas of beautiful country is so applicable to the Highlands, which were once also widely inhabited by a proud Gaelic-speaking race, many now banished to the New World. Someone wanting to buy or lease a ten-acre croft in a remote corner of the Highlands must first be subject to intense examination by the Crofters' Commission. Even if successful, they are still given no guarantee of ownership. Yet a wealthy foreigner may buy 100,000 acres of the most scenic part of Scotland with absolutely no control whatsoever. That this ludicrous and lamentable state of affairs is allowed to remain is a poignant illustration of the types of problems which have yet to be solved in Scotland. How many other countries allow their unique heritage to be bought and sold in this casual manner?

It is no accident that the last chapter of this book has dwelt totally on conservation, and starkly outlined some of the many problems and issues which exist. The future of Scotland's hills, and the Munros in particular, is intimately linked with these problems and issues and with any future conservation policies implemented as part of their solution. The Munro climber is a member of the largest and fastest-growing breed of a huge species of hillwalkers, backpackers, fell-runners, climbers and mountain-bikers who all crave the relaxation, peace and enchantment of the mountains. As such, the climber of Munros has an important part to play and is a crucial voice to be heard in any future discussions on Scotland's wild country. Today we can only hope that the peaceful tranquillity of these empty landscapes, watched over by the spirit of John Muir, will remain so indefinitely. Further, many have discovered, and many more have yet to discover, that wilderness is a necessity, and that after many thousands of years of escaping from the wild we are now returning to it or at least re-discovering its joys. This is perhaps best expressed in the words of John Muir: 'Thousands of tired, nerve-shaken, over-civilised people are beginning to find out that going to the mountains is going home.'

APPENDIX 1

The Tables Debate

A Bothy Conversation

Hughie: Aye, that was a grand day. That An Teallach's a braw mountain.

Archie: Aye, and just think – if we'd done the same ridge before 1981 we'd only have bagged one Munro and not two.

Hughie: Whit are you talkin' aboot?

Archie: Och, you probably wouldn't have remembered, but they revised Munro's Tables in 1981 and decided that An Teallach should have two Munros, and rightly so – Sgurr Fiona used to be just a Top.

Hughie: Wait a minute. Are you telling me someone's been tampering with Munro's Tables? Who's 'they' anyway?

Archie: Yon guy Hamish Brown that's done all the Munros about seven times and other people in the SMC.

Hughie: Aye, and does doin' the Munros seven times gie him the right to change Hugh Munro's Tables?

Archie: Maybe not – but you've got to admit that Sgurr Fiona is the main peak on the An Teallach ridge.

Hughie: Rubbish. Bidein a' Ghlas Thuill is three metres higher and it was the Munro and should be the only Munro.

Archie: So are you really saying that to do An Teallach you only have to climb Bidein a' Ghlas Thuill?

Hughie: Of course not. An Teallach is the whole ridge including Sgurr Fiona *and* the Corrag Bhuidhe pinnacles.

Archie: What about Glas Mheall Mor and Sail Liath?

Hughie: They're just Tops on either end of the ridge, but according to you Glas Mheall Mor could just as easily be a separate Munro – there's a good drop between it and Bidein a' Ghlas Thuill.

Archie: Aye, but it's no' really part of An Teallach.

Hughie: So what? Sgorr nam Fiannaidh's not part of Aonach Eagach but it's still a separate Munro.

Archie: Of course it is – it's the highest summit on the whole ridge.

Hughie: Agreed, but on Aonach Eagach itself there is only one Munro – Meall Dearg. Stob Coire Leith is still just a Top.

Archie: Aye, but there's very little height drop between the two. Look at Liathach. The distance and drop between Spidean a' Choire Leith and Mullach an Rathain is huge – they're now two separate Munros, and so they should be.

Hughie: How can you sit there and say that? If you start changing Munro's Tables they won't *be* Munro's Tables. Hugh Munro will be turning in his grave.

Archie: Come on, you're exaggerating here. Hugh Munro never kept to any definite guideline about the difference between Munros and Tops so the issue will always be subjective.

Hughie: Exactly, and the original list was subjective to him and if people start changing it they won't be Munros anymore. Where will it all end?

This fictitious discussion is typical of many which followed in the wake of the controversial Donaldson/Brown revision of Munro's Tables in 1981. The purpose of this appendix is not to pass judgement on anyone or take sides in the argument, but simply to throw light on the whole issue and let the reader adopt his or her own stance.

When people talk about 'the Munros' they generally mean the class of 277 separate mountains in Scotland which are 3,000 feet or over. There are, however, numerous other elevations over the 3,000-foot level which do not warrant 'separate-mountain' status as they are merely appendages or subsidiary summits linked to the main mountain. In the current edition of Munro's Tables there are in fact 517 Tops, which incidentally *include* the Munros as well. Someone who has *only* climbed the Munros still has another 240 summits to visit if he wishes to do all the Tops. In the original Tables published by Munro in 1891 there were 283 Munros and 538 Tops, and between then and now the numbers have shown significant variation.

This variation is largely due to the apparently subjective criterion which Munro adopted to distinguish between 'separate mountains' and 'Subsidiary Tops'. Of course, with successively more accurate surveying methods some mountains previously thought to be under 3,000 feet have been elevated to Munro status (and vice versa) and this has also produced a variation. It is also worth mentioning at this point that there is a third class of 3,000-foot elevations which do not even meet the requirement for Top status, comprising such obscure topographical features as shoulders, indeterminate wrinkles and other such undulations. When one looks at a map of Ben Avon in the Cairngorms with its diverse collection of satellite tops it becomes blatantly clear that the distinction between this latter group of summits and true Tops is more vague than the distinction between Tops and Munros. In fact, the Donaldson/Brown revision of 1981 reduced the number of Ben Avon's Tops from nine to four, and the total number of Tops deleted in the 1981 edition was 43. Seven Munros were also deleted, four new ones added and 19 new Tops also added.

These substantial changes were the biggest ever to be made (other than by Hugh Munro himself) in the course of the eight editions of the Tables which have appeared since their introduction in 1891. When Munro died in 1919 he was in the process of revising his list, and many anomalies remained in the 1921 edition, which was the first to incorporate Munro's changes.* Munro himself recognised the random nature of mountain status and made the comment: 'The exact number cannot be determined, owing to the impossibility of deciding what should be considered distinct mountains.'

Basically, all the revisions to Munro's Tables since 1891 have fallen into one of three categories. The first is that arising from a simple mistake or anomaly. The second arises from subsequent new height measurements which may indicate that a certain elevation is above or below 3,000 feet. The third, and most controversial, is that which stems from a purely personal viewpoint but which also may claim to have roots in Munro's methodology.

A good example of the first type is the listing in the 1891 Tables of Sgurr Dearg in the Skye Cuillin as a Munro and its partner the Inaccessible Pinnacle as only a Top, when in fact the Inaccessible Pinnacle is obviously the higher of the two. In fact, the 1891 Tables contain another seven such 'binary-pair' anomalies where the lower of the two twin summits is strangely accorded Munro status. It is difficult to account for these eight anomalies 'slipping through the net', and in particular the Sgurr Dearg example where the In. Pin. is so glaringly conspicuous as being the higher of the two. A glance at the OS map of today shows only Sgurr Dearg as the marked summit, and the presence of a name seemed to be an important condition for a Top to be considered as a separate mountain.

The second type of revision to the Tables is the least contentious, and there are many examples of new Munros being added because they have subsequently been found to exceed the magic 3,000-foot contour line. Similarly, a few have also been demoted. The most recent 'new Munro' was Beinn Teallach in Glen Spean, which was discovered to be over the height limit in 1984. Even more recent was the furore over the claims made about Foinaven in the far north being a Munro, but the argument seems to have settled in favour of it being below the required height. One particular peak, Beinn an Lochain near Arrochar, is probably suffering an identity crisis as it has jumped about from being a Munro to a Corbett on several occasions

* J.R. Young and A.W. Peacock were responsible for the 1921 revisions which produced 276 separate mountains.

– it was finally relegated to the Corbett ranks in the 1981 edition of the Tables. Several other peaks hover disconcertingly around the 3,000-foot mark, the most contentious of these being Sgurr a' Choire-bheithe in Knoydart (913m) and Beinn Dearg in Torridon (914m). Neither of these are Munros.

It is interesting (and confusing) that the lowest Munro, Beinn a' Chlaidheimh in the Fisherfield Forest, is also listed as being 914m in height. Yet 914m is only 2,998 feet. This serves to illustrate the extra problems which arose with the change from imperial to metric heights with the introduction of the new series of OS maps. Three thousand feet is almost halfway between 914m and 915m, and this, combined with the fact that the OS stubbornly refuse to show fractions of a metre, even in spot heights, gives a good indication of the types of problem which arise in trying to classify these borderline cases. Even the supposedly accurate satellite measurements of Foinaven still produced much controversy and confusion. The only certainty in all this is that there are bound to be subsequent additions and deletions on the basis of height alone, with continuing advances in measuring instruments.

We now move on to the third type of revision of the Tables which is characterised perfectly by the controversial Donaldson/Brown revisions of 1981 and was illustrated in the opening dialogue. It will be remembered that Hugh Munro offered no explanation of the basis of his classification of 3,000-foot mountains into Munros and Tops. Yet an analysis of the early Tables and some of the changes that Munro made give fairly thorough indications of at least some of the criteria he adopted in categorising the list. It was mentioned previously that the presence of a name influenced Munro's thinking. This was found to be the case with many double summits, as described earlier, although his 1921 revisions removed this particular anomaly and height rather than name took rightful priority.

However, a second example concerning names survived the 1921 revisions, showing almost conclusively that Munro was in favour of its retention, but in 1981 this case fell under the Donaldson/Brown hammer. The example concerns mountain groups with distinct *range names* such as Buachaille Etive Mor, Liathach, Beinn Eighe, An Teallach and Ben Wyvis. In each of these cases Hugh Munro assigned only one Munro, and none of the Tops in each range had the same name as the range. For example, the Liathach ridge contains no particular Top called Liathach, although it could be argued that Buachaille Etive Mor is really just another name for Stob Dearg.

On the other hand, other groups of mountains with *collective* names, such as the Mamores, the Grey Corries, the South Cluanie Ridge and the

Fannichs, all contain numerous Munros, despite the fact that the separation (in height and distance) between some Munros in these groups is less than that of some summits in the previous groups. Thus Munro himself clearly regarded ranges such as Liathach and An Teallach to be single mountains and hence to contain only one Munro. They both now contain two Munros each in the wake of the 1981 changes. Yet mighty Beinn Eighe, with its magnificent cluster of six distinct 3,000-foot summits, was curiously left alone with its one Munro of Ruadh-stac Mor; certainly the highest summit, but rather a whale-back outlier lying off the main ridge. If any mountain in Scotland had a claim to having more than one Munro, it was Beinn Eighe – Spidean Coire nan Clach and Sail Mhor deserve Munro status more than many a summit on the South Cluanie Ridge. Even assuming the validity of Donaldson and Brown's revisions, their omission of Beinn Eighe highlights a gross inconsistency in standards and one which stands out with painful clarity.

At this point, however, it should be stressed that Brown and Donaldson were only cogs (albeit important cogs) in the much greater SMC 'machine' which pile-drove the changes through, leaving the current bickering and dissatisfaction.

Owing to their vast 'hands-on' experience of Munros, Brown and Donaldson were asked by the SMC to recommend some revisions in the wake of map metrication and the OS re-survey. The recommended revisions were then discussed with the SMC at a meeting and finally put to the vote. The result, in Hamish Brown's own words, was 'a botched-up compromise', which he himself was clearly unhappy with. On discussing the issue with Hamish, he had no hesitation in remarking that the SMC lost a unique chance to do the job properly.

Returning to the obvious test case of Beinn Eighe, with its two conspicuous contenders of Sail Mhor and Spidean Coire nan Clach, it was pointed out that the promotion of only one of these to Munro status would have constituted a greater inconsistency than promoting neither. Yet would it? The Tops are two miles apart on almost opposite ends of the main ridge (ignoring the Tops east of Spidean Coire nan Clach), but in particular this latter Top, at 993m, is the second highest in the whole range with a drop of well over 150m between it and the Munro of Ruadh-stac Mor. In other words, even applying the strict 500-feet-of-re-ascent criterion adopted for Corbetts, Spidean Coire nan Clach still makes the grade. Moreover, the name Beinn Eighe applies to this Top more than any other one in the range – it is the most distinctive and representative summit in the group. Yet, despite all this, full Munro status still eludes it.

The argument for Sail Mhor is certainly not as convincing, it being third highest in the range and having a drop of around 120m between it and

Ruadh-stac Mor. Sail Mhor stands proud, however, at the true western termination of the Beinn Eighe Ridge and is more deserving than many a Munro on the South Cluanie Ridge.

However, the logical proposal of three Munros for Beinn Eighe led to an outcry among the ranks of the SMC. The addition of a second Munro to An Teallach and Liathach was palatable but to add *two* Munros to Beinn Eighe was going too far. Surely the obvious compromise of promoting Spidean Coire nan Clach would have been the patent and natural alternative? But it was not to be, and for the moment anyway we are stuck with what many (including Hamish Brown) see as an unfortunate half-measure.

Furthermore, the arguments do not end here (although Beinn Eighe does present the most painful anomaly). Further down the glen the jewel of Beinn Alligin contains only one Munro (Sgurr Mhor) on its fine horseshoe ridge. The subsidiary Top of Tom na Gruagaich has a full 155m drop between it and the parent summit, and therefore by Corbett's criterion the ridge would contain two Corbetts. Perhaps in some future edition of Munro's Tables this Top, together with Beinn Eighe's two contenders, will have gained rightful promotion to establish a tidy list of 280 Munros which the majority of people will be happy with. The adoption of a partial Corbett criterion which promotes to full Munro status any Top satisfying the '500-foot rule' (but not relegating existing Munros which don't) may well turn out to be the most logical solution to the ongoing dilemma. This would produce only one other contender for promotion: the Top of Stob Coire Raineach on Buachaille Etive Beag, making a not-so-tidy 281 Munros.

Hamish Brown himself admits that the present situation could easily change in the future – his only complaint at the moment is that he is taking all the bad press and flak for an inconsistency which is ultimately attributable to the SMC as a whole. His sense of humour prevails, however, when he makes the remark that it 'serves all those hillwalkers right who had only done one Munro on An Teallach and Liathach before the revisions in 1981'. And can someone really claim to have done Beinn Eighe having only climbed Ruadh-stac Mor?

Some would say that far from removing anomalies from Munro's Tables, the 1981 revisions have actually created more, and the introduction of many new Tops, together with even more deletions, has confused the issue further. Hugh Munro's words of wisdom spoken in 1891 sum up the whole debate: 'The decision as to what are to be considered distinct and separate mountains, and what maybe counted as 'tops', although arrived at after careful consideration, cannot be finally insisted on.' In a sense, these words create a dichotomy. On one hand, Munro is saying that there will always be summits whose Munro/Top status is arguable and therefore he is leaving the issue open for future changes to be made (as in the 1981 revisions). On the other hand, he has already passed judgement on the status of the summits (subjective as it may be), and by identifying his name with the list of Scottish 3,000-foot peaks we have a moral duty to preserve his list.

Several people have made attempts at rationalising Munro's classification or at providing a logical alternative. In particular, Frank Bonsall of the SMC used the measure of the time taken to walk to any higher point (based on Naismith's Rule) and this may possibly have formed the basis of the 1981 revisions, although as we have seen the job was not fully completed. J. Gall Inglis, another SMC member, suggested a 75–100-foot height differential between connecting col and summit as a way of distinguishing between Tops. Dane Love recently provided a substantial, logical alternative to Munro's list by removing the distinction between Mountains and Tops. He chose to call them *all* mountains and used a criterion of a drop of at least 100 feet between two summits. On this basis, Love arrived at a list which draws interesting parallels with Munro's list – 425 of Love's mountains are also Munro mountains or Tops.

Since metrication of OS maps, a few individuals have made brave suggestions of metricating Munros and have, not surprisingly, met with fierce opposition. A list of all Scottish mountains over 1,000m may present a nice tidy list, but these 135 mountains and 229 Tops could certainly not be called Munros. The other suggestion of trimming the 914m limit to a neat 900m would certainly retain the 'old' Munros but introduce 21 other peaks which are presently known as Corbetts, bringing the total to 298 'Munros'. However, the definition of a Corbett as a Scottish mountain over 2,500 feet has the additional qualification of having a 500-foot drop on all sides and so the two lists are not comparable. On a rough Munro rationale there would be over 300 mountains above the 900m contour. Either way, the resulting list would not be a list of Munros as envisaged by Sir Hugh Munro. Further discussion on mountain lists can be found in Chapter 9.

The purpose of this appendix is simply to throw light on the more controversial aspects of the Munro/Top dichotomy. Admittedly, the reader may feel even more confused at this point, but it therefore follows that he or she has at least become aware of just how complex the whole issue is. One thing is certain and that is that discussion and argument will persist into the future. If Hugh Munro were alive today he would no doubt be chuckling to himself in amazement as to how serious the problems of his innocent list have become – in some people's minds. Whether you climb today's list, yesterday's list, new Munros, demoted Munros or your own list, the real message of Munro is to enjoy the adventure, exploration and challenge, but above all have fun.

APPENDIX 2

The Safety Debate

A Pub Conversation

Wullie: I see there's been another two folk killed on the mountains this weekend – that's about ten this year already.

Maggie: Aye, and they've naebody to blame but themselves. Whit people in their right minds go oot to the mountains in the middle o' winter?

Wullie: Well, me for one – and I enjoy it.

Maggie: Aye, well we ken you're no' in your right mind anyway – I'm talking aboot *normal* people.

Wullie: Look, there's thousands of people go out to the hills in winter – they can't all be wrong.

Maggie: Well there's ten wrong this year already – that proves it's helluva dangerous.

Wullie: Rubbish. If you take the necessary precautions like wearing crampons and carrying an ice-axe it's no' any more dangerous than in summer.

Maggie: Aye, so how come a' these people are fa'n off mountains?

Wullie: Well it says here one of them didnae have crampons and the other did, and the one without slipped. His mate with the crampons tried to stop him and . . .

Maggie: Ach I'm no' interested in all this crampon stuff – what aboot all these dipsticks that are doin' the Munros, they're the real idiots.

Wullie: They *were* climbing Munros! Hillwalkers wear crampons and carry ice-axes too, you know. It's not just climbers that have all the gear.

Maggie: Aye, well I reckon they should ban people from the hills in winter – it would save a lot of lives, including the mountain-rescue people.

Wullie: Maggie, you're talking through a hole in your head. [*Or words to that effect.*] Just how do you propose to stop people climbing hills in winter? Fine them? Lock them up? Place guards at every Munro? The idea is ludicrous.

Maggie: Maybe, but look at the risk, they're puttin' these mountain-rescue people to – why should they have to go out and rescue some stupid bugger stuck halfway up a cliff-face?

Wullie: Look, they don't *have* to go and rescue people; they do it because they want to – they're all volunteers, they don't even get paid for it.

Maggie: That's no' the point. Their lives are still being put at risk through the irresponsible actions of others.

Wullie: Maggie, listen. Many mountain-rescue volunteers were climbers or are climbers themselves. They understand what makes people want to go to the mountains, and they also understand that they themselves might one day need to be rescued so there's a kind of friendly community relationship between climbers and rescuers. Help one another is the name of the game.

Maggie: That's all very well but what about the *really* irresponsible people who go out without a map or a compass or climb Ben Nevis with trainers, a T-shirt and no rucksack. They really don't deserve to get rescued.

Wullie: Come on! You can't just leave them up there – that would be callous and even more irresponsible.

Maggie: Right, so you do agree that some people are irresponsible in the first place and are needlessly putting other people's lives at risk.

Wullie: I agree that some people are less responsible than others but they don't need shouted at, they need to be educated and shown the right direction as far as safety is concerned.

Maggie: Aye, well anyway it's your round.

This is probably fairly typical of the discussions which usually follow in the aftermath of a series of tragic incidents in the mountains. As in the first appendix, the purpose of this section is not to play God and uphold any particular viewpoint but to give the whole issue of safety and rescue a good airing and explain the crucial relevance to the rising Munro phenomenon. It should also open the eyes of present and potential Munro-baggers to the importance of safety.

It is a common misconception among non-mountaineers that the majority of accidents in the hills happen to those who are engaged in technical climbing as opposed to plain hillwalking. The truth is, in fact, the exact opposite: the bulk of incidents involve walkers rather than climbers. A well-equipped, roped climber with much experience on a steep, icy face is in a safer position than a relatively inexperienced walker blundering about without crampons on hard névé (tightly packed snow) and daylight fading fast. This example may appear to give the impression that all walkers are inexperienced and irresponsible, which is not the case. What is true is that there are more inexperienced walkers than inexperienced climbers and hence more accidents befall walkers. The simple explanation for why there are more inexperienced walkers is that there are more walkers. However, it is not just a case of different proportions: the fraction of climbers who have accidents is extremely small indeed – much smaller than the fraction of walkers who have accidents. The reason for this is that climbers are generally very aware of the inherent dangers and of the equipment needed; they have to be, for the simple reason that the *potential* danger they flirt with is far greater than that of hillwalkers. Thus we have reached the ironic conclusion that the largest group of hill-users (including Munro-baggers) who deal with the smallest amount of potential danger have many more accidents than the group who deal with the most potential danger.

Yet it is precisely this minimum potential danger which builds up a false sense of security in the novice hillwalker and urges him or her on to attempt feats which may ultimately result in tragedy. This false sense of security may also include a lowering of one's guard, especially when descending a hill in a tired condition, when a simple slip can result in tragic consequences. A slip is the most common cause of mountain accidents.

It is informative but alarming to note the general trend of accident statistics over a period of years, and in particular those resulting in death. In 1985 the number of fatalities was 18 but by 1991 the number had risen dramatically to 41. In the space of just six years the number of people killed annually on the Scottish mountains more than doubled. In fact, the first three months of 1991 saw over 21 deaths, of which 15 happened in less than a month. The beginning of 1993 also proved deadly, with 15 people killed before the end of February. In 1994, 19 were killed before the end of March . . .

What can we learn from these gruesome statistics? It is revealing that 13 of the 15 people killed at the beginning of 1993 were engaged in the simple act of hillwalking at the time of the accident. At least ten of these 13 died as a result of a slip either on névé or on ice. It would be easy to dismiss these slips as being simply attributable to chance stumblings or momentary carelessness and leave it there. However, this is certainly not the whole story, and further probing reveals that the real reason for these accidents can be traced back to three root causes, which are not necessarily mutually exclusive. The first and most basic is the lack of necessary equipment, such as ice-axe and crampons to cope with hard snow and ice. The second is being in possession of the equipment but failing to have the necessary experience and expertise to use it properly – the Liathach Ridge is not a good place to learn how to walk with crampons or practise ice-axe arrest. The third cause is the most indirect but also the most fundamental in the sense that it can lead to situations where a slip is more likely to happen. According to John Hinde, the accident recorder for the mountain-rescue committee of Scotland, poor navigation contributes to about half of all accidents on Scotland's mountains. If a hillwalker is not sure of his whereabouts then he is more likely to wander on to ground which he is not equipped to cope with, especially if visibility is poor.

A combination of these three causes led to the tragic deaths of three members of the Mayo family in the Cairngorms in February 1993. Dr Christopher Mayo, his son Matthew and his brother Michael were hillwalking in the Coire an Lochain area when they mistakenly strayed on to steep, icy slopes. One adult is thought to have slipped and fallen almost 1,000 feet to the corrie below. The other adult left to raise the alarm, leaving Matthew in an ice cave inside a survival bag. However, after only a short distance the second adult also fell. Both men died from multiple injuries and intense cold, while Matthew later died from hypothermia. It was later discovered that none of the group had crampons, only one had rigid-sole boots and only one ice-axe was available between them.

It is easy for the gloom merchants, like Maggie in the opening dialogue, to point the finger and make accusations or ludicrous, unworkable suggestions such as closing the mountains off in winter. The reality is that with the continuing surge of weekend Munro-baggers there are bound to be more accidents, simply by the laws of statistics. In the wake of multiple tragedies on the mountains some people are driven to adopting extreme attitudes, like the call for the demolition of Jean's hut and the Curran Bothy in the Cairngorms – both have been removed. It was while trying to reach the Curran Bothy in November 1971 that five teenage schoolchildren and an 18-year-old trainee instructor died of exposure at an emergency bivouac only 500 yards from the bothy. The Curran Bothy became an innocent victim of this tragic event. The logical upshot of this act would be to destroy all forms of man-made shelter in the hills. Other extremists have called for access to the Cairngorm plateau to be denied from October to April, or a height of 2,000 feet to be the maximum allowed, and routes of ascent to be also routes of return.

In the final analysis, there is little to be done but accept the fact that more people are going to the hills and try to impress on them a need to be safety conscious. In addition to learning how to use a map and compass and practising with crampons and ice-axe, there is also the question of approaching the sport with the right attitude. Too many hillwalkers are becoming blinkered by climbing Munros to the extent that safety takes a back seat. A deterioration in weather may make the ascent of a lower hill (possibly a non-Munro) a more viable proposition, yet many are not flexible enough to change plans or modify a route in the light of changed circumstances. The 'carry-on-regardless' mentality is fine up to a point; experience is knowing when that point has been reached. This works both ways – some novice hillwalkers will want to retreat at the slightest inkling of bad weather; others may battle on in a raging blizzard. The experienced hillwalker reaches a happy medium based on a multitude of other similar situations. As Hamish Brown is fond of remarking, 'Experience is the sum of near misses.'

The 'safety-in-numbers' syndrome is partly a fallacy, as a large group of people climbing a mountain can create a false sense of security. If there is no natural leader in the group the situation can soon become farcical when the weather worsens. Each member of the group will continue to plod along, imagining that someone else will make the decision to retreat or carry on. It is worth mentioning at this point that the number of accidents befalling solo hillwalkers is surprisingly low. A solo hillwalker *has* to have confidence in himself on the hill; if he doesn't he probably won't be around for too long. Of course, the combination of company *and* experience is the best recipe for staying alive on the hill.

It is known that a large percentage of accidents happen to people from south of the border. This does not imply that the English are somehow inherently less capable of climbing mountains safely (although some would disagree!). Quite simply, on any particular weekend the proportion of English people on the hills is very high and therefore statistically we should expect a high proportion of accidents. However, there is also the fact that they have travelled much further to reach a particular mountain or range of mountains, and are correspondingly less inclined to turn round and go home if the weather is bad. Someone who has driven 500 miles just to climb Bidean Nam Bian in Glencoe is less likely to be put off by bad weather than someone who has only driven 50 miles. There also exists the plain fact that the Scots are more used to bad weather and more likely to ascertain the possibility of its fluctuations than the English.

We now turn to an invaluable service which was discussed in the opening dialogue, and without which there would certainly be many more fatalities on the Scottish mountains. The mountain-rescue service was developed in the post-war years using helicopters based at Leuchars and Lossiemouth, the former using Wessex and the latter using Sea-King helicopters. Those 'in the know' will no doubt realise that the Leuchars helicopters were withdrawn from use at the end of March 1993 following government cutbacks. This controversial decision has unleashed much passionate debate and the general consensus of opinion is that a backward step has been taken. Wessex helicopters are known to be highly manoeuvrable in mountainous terrain and have saved many lives, as well as providing valuable training for the RAF pilots and rescuers. However,

A rescue helicopter
in the Lost Valley,
Glencoe

renowned mountaineer and leader of the Glencoe Mountain Rescue Team Hamish MacInnes believes that Sea Kings are no worse than Wessexes, although there are now fewer helicopters available.

The real reason for mentioning the withdrawal of the Leuchars helicopters is to highlight the perennial and underlying problem of finance affecting mountain search and rescue. Although the government provides much of the funding for these helicopters, the mountain-rescue services themselves are an entirely voluntary body whose only source of income is from appeals, donations from wellwishers and the media, and other such contributions. Many individuals view this set-up as an outdated state of affairs and believe that Britain is behind the rest of Europe as far as rescue services go. However, the voluntary arrangement here is actually the envy of many European countries and, besides, the mountain-rescue committees, like the lifeboat institution, have a long-established tradition of voluntary service which works extremely well.

There are those who believe that helicopter and rescue services should be funded completely from insurance, which is essentially the case in Europe. This would require all mountaineers, from casual summer hillwalkers to winter ice climbers, to take out special mountaineering insurance, without which they could not be rescued unless an extremely large amount of money was forthcoming! The 'Maggies' of this world would no doubt agree with such an arrangement, arguing that if people come to grief on the mountains through their own misadventure then they should accordingly pay the penalty – either with their wallets or their lives. This rather dispassionate viewpoint is probably more in favour with non-mountaineers than with mountaineers, but it certainly appears to have much to commend it. Yet the intricacies of its instigation and operation would be a minefield for insurance companies, with all sorts of bizarre scenarios presenting themselves. Would an injured climber have to produce proof of his insurance before being airlifted off? Who pays if it is subsequently discovered that he is not insured? Would there be different premiums payable for walkers and climbers? Who should pay the most?

It is fairly evident that if such an insurance scheme ever comes about it will be many years into the future. One unique group who hope and believe that such a move will never materialise is the recently formed Boots Across Scotland Trust Fund, which in May 1988 and June 1992 hoped to have at least one person standing at the summit of every Munro in Scotland at exactly the same time. The idea was the brainchild of Gordon Pierson, who, following a close shave on Buachaille Etive Mor, realised just how close he had been to becoming another casualty. More importantly, his close friend 'Big Davy' Pearson was in a wheelchair, bravely coping with occupational therapy following a horrific fall from the Etive Slabs in Glen Etive. Luckily, he had been picked up by a rescue helicopter and rushed to hospital for prolonged treatment.

Gordon Pierson, and many other climbers and hillwalkers, are acutely aware of how easily accidents can happen, and it was Gordon's idea to organise simultaneous sponsored climbs of all the Munros in order to raise money for Big Davy and others like him. Thus the Boots Across Scotland Trust Fund was born, becoming one of the most touching outdoor fund-raising events in Britain.

The 1988 event was marred by a single tragically ironic incident which threatened to overshadow the whole venture. While participating in an event organised to help save lives, one volunteer slipped and fell on the Tarmachan Ridge, losing his life. There was a double irony present in that the adverse publicity created by this tragic occurrence helped attract more fund-raising potential. The happy ending to the 1988 saga saw the initial target of £20,000 almost quadrupled – £75,000 was raised for the Glasgow Mountain Rescue team and Stobhill Hospital in Glasgow.

However, Boots Across Scotland is not only concerned with fund-raising but also aims to provide sensible advice and safety education to the growing band of people heading for the Scottish hills. Prevention of accidents is their core objective and almost 3,000 individuals have attended hill-safety lectures organised by them and mountaineer Mick Tighe. Navigation, first-aid and winter skill courses are now also arranged with special help for handicapped people. It is to be hoped that Boots will continue to flourish in the years to come – it certainly deserves to.

Before concluding this important appendix, it is salutary to mention one characteristic which all experienced mountaineers possess, but which covers a wide range of knowledge, skills and practice: that of mountain-sense. This seemingly loosely defined phrase encompasses such diverse abilities as reading the weather and making decisions based on this, understanding the lie of the land, knowing by sight what is with or beyond the limitations of self or group, knowing when to alter a route or make a retreat and generally having a feel for the mountain based on a solid foundation of experience in all weathers. Mountain-sense does not entail technical knowledge but 'only' an awareness of the mountain, the weather, the terrain and likelihood of potential danger. Like road-sense, mountain-sense is the knack of being perpetually conscious of what lies ahead and having the wherewithal to make correct decisions, and act on those decisions when necessary.

It has been said that the best way of learning road-sense is to ride a bicycle or motorcycle. What is the best way of learning mountain-sense? The answer is simply by undertaking plenty of hillwalks of varying standard, duration and weather conditions, including winter outings. Munro-bagging is ideal. There exists a common fallacy that hillwalking requires no technique and that nothing is really learned from it. In fact, it requires a great deal, and all hillwalkers, experienced or inexperienced, continue to absorb a whole variety of useful, though sometimes subconscious bits of knowledge which last a lifetime. The late J.H.B. Bell, highly regarded mountaineer and SMC member, regarded hillwalking as central to mountaineering:

> 'Hillwalking is true mountaineering, however the hard-bitten rock-climber may regard it. Walking is the head and cornerstone of all mountain-climbing, whether we are dealing with the little 1,000-foot hill near our homes or taking part in an assault on an unclimbed 20,000-foot giant of the Himalaya. In certain kinds of weather and atmospheric lighting, the one can look almost as beautiful and impressive as the other.'

Finally, just to hammer home the continuing need for safety on the mountains, here is an interesting though alarming statistic. In the first 41 years of the Scottish Mountaineering Club only one person was killed on the Scottish mountains. In 1991 alone 41 people were killed. The words of Alpine climber Edward Whymper could not be bettered to end this appendix:

> Climb if you will, but remember that courage and strength are nought without prudence, and that a momentary negligence may destroy the happiness of a lifetime. Do nothing in haste; look well to each step; and from the beginning think what might be the end.

APPENDIX 3

Facts and Figures

A Munro Calendar of Events Since 1891

1891	The first edition of Munro's Tables appears in the *SMC Journal*.
1894	Hugh Munro is elected president of the SMC.
1901	The Revd A.E. Robertson becomes the first person to climb all the Munros (the first Munroist).
1919	Sir Hugh Munro dies, aged 63.
1921	The SMC publishes its *General Guide* with Hugh Munro's revised and updated list of 3,000-foot mountains.
1923	The Revd A. Burns becomes the second Munroist and the first person to also complete all the Tops.
1929	J.A. Parker becomes the first person to complete all the Munros *and* 3,000-foot peaks in England, Wales and Ireland (Furth).
1947	Mrs J. Hirst becomes the first woman to complete all the Munros (and Tops). Mr and Mrs J. Hirst also become the first married couple to complete.
1949	W.M. Docharty becomes the first person to complete all the Munros, Tops *and* Furth – known as the Grand Slam.
1960	Miss Anne Littlejohn becomes the first woman to complete the Grand Slam.
1964	Philip Tranter completes a *second* round of the Munros and climbs a record 19 Munros in 24 hours.
1965	W.A. Poucher's *The Scottish Peaks* is published.
1967	The first attempt at a continuous traverse of all the Munros by the Ripley brothers. 230 Munros are completed.
1974	The first successful continuous, self-propelled traverse of all the Munros by Hamish Brown in 112 days (described in *Hamish's Mountain Walk*).
1978	Charlie Ramsay climbs 24 Munros in 24 hours (Ramsay's Round)
1981	Publication of new edition of Munro's Tables with the controversial Donaldson/Brown revisions.
1982	Kathy Murgatroyd makes the first continuous round of the Munros by a woman and the second continuous round, taking 134 days

1984   The first continuous round of the Munros and English and Welsh 3,000-footers in 165 days by George Keeping (entirely on foot).

1984/85   The first (and only) winter round of the Munros in 83 days by Martin Moran (vehicle assisted) (described in *The Munros in Winter*).

1985   The SMC guide *The Munros* is published.

1985/86   The first (and only) continuous round of the Munros and Corbetts in 13 months by Craig Caldwell (described in *Climb Every Mountain*).

1986   Irvine Butterfield's *The High Mountains* is published.

1986   Ashley Cooper makes the first continuous round of the Munros and Furth.

1987   Martin Stone extends Ramsay's Round and climbs 26 Munros in 24 hours.

1988   Mark Elsegood completes the Munros in 66 days with the help of a car.

Jon Broxap climbs 28 Munros in 24 hours in the Shiel/Affric area.

The first Boots Across Scotland event aims for a simultaneous climb of all the Munros on 1 May.

1989   Paul Tattersall makes the first continuous round of the Munros while on or carrying a mountain-bike.

1990   The fastest continuous traverse of the Munros and Furth in 97 days by Hugh Symonds; also including the fastest purely self-propelled round of the Munros in 67 days (entirely on foot and no ferries used) (see also 1994).

A team of seven fell runners complete the Munros by relay in under 13 days.

Stuart Clements and Kate Weyman become the first couple to accomplish a continuous round of the Munros.

1991   *The Munro Show* appears on Scottish Television.

The Munro Almanac by Cameron McNeish is published.

Centenary dinner held in the Roxburghe Hotel, Edinburgh.

Adrian Belton climbs 28 Munros in 24 hours in the Lochaber area (an extension to Ramsay's Round).

1992   Andrew Johnstone and Rory Gibson complete the Munros in a record 51 days.

1993   A team of seven fell-runners complete the Munros by relay in 11 days 20 hours.

1994   Mike Cudahy completes the Munros in 66 days and 7 hours entirely on foot (but using ferries).

Some Notable Facts

The bulk of the following information was correct on 1 August 1994 and any subsequent updates are not included. Most details have been gleaned from the *SMC Journal* and are only based on known official records.

Numbers

The number of Munroists is 1,274, of which 257 have also completed the Tops and 188 Furth.

The number of 'Grand Slammers' (Munros, Tops and Furth) is 109.

The number of female Munroists is 175 (only about 14% of all Munroists are female).

The number of married couples finishing together is 47.

The number of families of four finishing together is 2 (the Morgans in 1985 and the Kales in 1987).

Records

The *fastest* round of the Munros was completed by Andrew Johnstone and Rory Gibson in 1992, taking 51 days.

The *slowest* round of the Munros was finally completed in 1989 by Iain Ogilvie, who took 64 years. He climbed his first Munro at the age of 14 and, owing to long periods working abroad, did not climb his last until he was 78, which is the *greatest age* for completion.

The *youngest* Munroist is David Kale, who was 13 years and 10 months on completion (of the Kale family above).

The *oldest* surviving Munroist on record is Ivan Waller, born in 1906, who was 73 years old on completion and was 88 in 1994.

The *earliest* visit to a Munro summit was that of Mark Waugh, who was born in the cabin of a helicopter during a snowstorm on the summit of An Riabhachan!

The *most* Munros completed in a day is 28 by Jon Broxap in 1988 in the Shiel/Affric area, and also by Adrian Belton in 1991 in Lochaber.

The *greatest* number of complete Munro rounds is seven (including two with a dog), by Hamish Brown between 1968 and 1984.

The *greatest* number of complete Munro rounds by a woman is five (including three rounds of the Tops) by Geraldine Howie.

The *most* Munros climbed in the *shortest* time is 11 in 3 hours 32 minutes by Andy Hyslop on the Cuillin Ridge. (This is the current Cuillin Ridge record.)

A Brief note on skiing

The two disciplines of Nordic skiing and Alpine ski-mountaineering as a method of traversing mountainous country in winter have been long

Two pictures of three of the Morgan family (Mr Paul Morgan, Mrs Barbara Morgan, Gareth and Caroline), who between the years of 1980 and 1985 climbed all the Munros as a complete family – one of only two families to have done so

established in Scotland. The first traverse of the four 4,000-foot Cairngorm Munros in 1953 by Norman Clark was something of a landmark event, and since then many mountaineers have become addicted to ski-mountaineering.

The finest long-distance ski-tour in Scotland is known as the 'Scottish Haute Route', an idea stemming from the famous Alpine Haute Route from Chamonix to Zermatt. The route runs 100 miles from the eastern Cairngorms to Ben Nevis and requires a week of settled weather and good snow cover – an unlikely scenario. After many attempts, the traverse was accomplished by David Grieve and Mike Taylor in March 1978.

The ultimate challenge of a continuous Munro traverse on skis is not really a viable proposition when one thinks of the Skye Cuillin, An Teallach or Aonach Eagach; although in the winter of 1989, Peter Nichol of the Caithness Mountaineering and Ski Club spent six weeks skiing over the major groups of Munros, starting at Ben Lomond and finishing on Ben Hope.

Continuous Munro Rounds

The following is a list of people who are *known* to have completed a continuous round of the Munros with or without vehicular back-up. Obviously, the list cannot claim to be comprehensive as there may exist cases of unpublished continuous rounds. (Anyone who has completed a continuous round and is not on this list, please send your name and address to Andrew Dempster, c/o Mainstream Publishing Co. Ltd and you should appear in the next edition of this book.) Although no official definition of what is meant by a continuous Munro round exists, for sake of argument anyone completing all the Munros within the space of six months can be said to have made a continuous round, regardless of whether they go home for a few days' rest or lie on a beach for a week halfway through their quest! This could be regarded as a list of 'super-Munroists'.

1.	Hamish Brown	1974
2.	Kathy Murgatroyd	1982
3.	George Keeping	1984 (including English and Welsh 3,000-footers)
4.	Martin Moran	1984–85
5.	Craig Caldwell	1985–86 (including the Corbetts)
6.	Ashley Cooper	1986 (including Furth)
7.	Mike Cawthorne	1986
8.	Mark Elsegood	1988
9.	Mike Wilson-Roberts	1989
10.	Paul Tattersall	1989

11.	Hugh Symonds	1990 (including Furth)
12.	Stuart Clements	1990
13.	Kate Weyman	1990
14.	Andrew Johnstone	1992
15.	Rory Gibson	1992
16.	Mike Cudahy	1994

It is interesting and almost strange that no one has yet attempted all the Munros and Tops in a single expedition, though like the inclusion of the Corbetts this would involve a much-extended itinerary and would probably be a 'one-off'. The ultimate challenge could be considered to be the 'continuous Grand Slam', i.e. all the Munros, Tops and Furth in a single trip. It is not unlikely that this monumental challenge will be tackled before the end of the century. For the real masochists out there, the Corbetts could also be thrown in! Beyond this, the only restriction is the imagination. By all means dream dreams but sometimes set them free and put feet to the wings of vision.

> *Farewell, ye forests of the heath, hills where the bright day gleams,*
> *Farewell, ye grassy dells, farewell, ye springs and leaping streams,*
> *Farewell, ye mighty solitudes, where once I loved to dwell –*
> *Scenes of my spring-time and its joys – for ever fare you well.*
>
> Duncan Ban MacIntyre, 'Last Farewell to the Hills'

BIBLIOGRAPHY AND GUIDE TO
FURTHER READING

Bell, J.H.B., *Bell's Scottish Climbs*, Gollancz, 1988

Bennet, D. (editor), *The Munros*, SMT, 1985

Bennet, D. and Wallace, W., *Ski Mountaineering in Scotland*, SMT, 1987

Borthwick, A., *Always a Little Further*, Diadem, 1983 (republished)

Brooker, W.D. (editor), *A Century of Scottish Mountaineering*, SMT, 1988

Brown, H.M., *Climbing the Corbetts*, Gollancz, 1988

Brown, H.M., *Hamish's Mountain Walk*, Gollancz, 1978

Brown, H.M. (editor), *Poems of the Scottish Hills*, Aberdeen University Press, 1982

Butterfield, I., *The High Mountains of Britain and Ireland*, Diadem, 1986

Caldwell, C., *Climb Every Mountain*, Macdonald, 1990

Clark, R.W. and Pyatt, E.C., *Mountaineering in Britain*, Phoenix, 1957

Dawson A., *The Relative Hills of Britain*, Cicerone, 1992

Docharty, W., *A Selection of Some 900 British and Irish Tops* (3 volumes), private publication, 1954

Donaldson, J. and Brown, H.M. (editors), *Munro's Tables*, SMC, 1990

Drummond, P. and Mitchell, I., *The First Munroist*, Ernest Press, 1993

Dutton, G.J.F., *The Ridiculous Mountains*, Diadem, 1994

Dutton, G.J.F., *Nothing So Simple as Climbing*, Diadem, 1993

Gilbert, R., *Memorable Munros*, Diadem, 1983

Gray, M., *The First Fifty, Munro Bagging Without a Beard*, Mainstream, 1991

Hewitt, Dave, *Walking the Watershed*, Tacit Press, 1994

Humble, B.H., *The Cuillin of Skye*, Ernest Press, 1986

Johnstone, S., Brown, H.M. and Bennet, D. (editors), *The Corbetts and Other Scottish Hills*, SMT, 1990

Moran, M., *The Munros in Winter*, David and Charles, 1986

Moran, M., *Scotland's Winter Mountains*, David and Charles, 1988

Murray, W.H., *Mountaineering in Scotland / Undiscovered Scotland*, Diadem, 1982

Murray, W.H., *Scotland's Mountains*, SMT, 1987

Patey, T., *One Man's Mountains*, Gollancz, 1986

Poucher, W.A., *The Scottish Peaks*, Constable, 1965

Steven, C., *The Story of Scotland's Hills*, Hale, 1975

Symonds, H., *Running High*, Lochar, 1991

Weir, T., *Highland Days*, Gordon Wright, 1948, 1984

Weir, T., *Tom Weir's Scotland*, Gordon Wright, 1980

Numerous *SMC Journal*s 1891–1994

INDEX OF NAMES